HOW TO
WRITE FOR
TELEVISION

If you want to know how. . .

Getting Into Films & Television
*How to spot the opportunities
and find the best way in*

How to Get a Job in Television
*Insider secrets you need to know to get
and keep your dream job in TV*

Working in the Music Industry
*How to find an exciting and varied career
in the world of music*

Creative Writing
*Unlock your imagination, develop your writing skills,
and get your work published*

howtobooks

Please send for a free copy of the latest catalogue:

How To Books
Spring Hill House, Spring Hill Road
Begbroke, Oxford OX5 1RX, United Kingdom
email: info@howtobooks.co.uk
http://www.howtobooks.co.uk

HOW TO WRITE FOR TELEVISION

A guide to writing and selling successful TV scripts

REVISED AND UPDATED
5TH
FIFTH EDITION

WILLIAM SMETHURST

howto books

Published by How To Books Ltd,
Spring Hill House, Spring Hill Road,
Begbroke, Oxford OX5 1RX. United Kingdom.
Tel: (01865) 375794. Fax: (01865) 379162
info@howtobooks.co.uk
www.howtobooks.co.uk

First published 2000
Second edition 2002
Third edition 2004
Fourth edition 2005
Fifth edition 2007

British Library Cataloguing in Publication Data
A catalogue record for this book is available from the British
Library

ISBN: 978 1 84528 181 6

Cover design by Baseline Arts Ltd, Oxford
Produced for How To Books by Deer Park Productions, Tavistock
Typeset by PDQ Typesetting, Newcastle-under-Lyme
Printed and bound by Cromwell Press, Trowbridge, Wiltshire

NOTE: The material contained in this book is set out in good
faith for general guidance and no liability can be accepted
for loss or expense incurred as a result of relying in particular
circumstances on statements made in the book. The laws and
regulations are complex and liable to change, and readers should
check the current position with the relevant authorities before
making personal arrangements.

Contents

List of Illustrations

The Opportunities

TELEVISION NEEDS *YOU*!

Television is desperately short of writers. Once there was just BBC 1 and ITV 1, and the only soap opera was *Coronation Street*. Now there are five terrestrial channels and a host of digital channels like BBC3 and BBC4, and instead of *Coronation Street* just twice a week there's now also *Eastenders*, and *Emmerdale*, and *Hollyoaks* for teenagers, and *Doctors* in the afternoons – all putting out three, four, or five episodes a week.

All these programmes – and the series like *Heartbeat, Holby City, The Royal*, need scriptwriters, and scriptwriters are increasingly in short supply. A good new writer on *Casualty*? Word flies round the industry, and before you know it the writer concerned is doing an episode of *The Bill* and the *Casualty* script editors are bitterly complaining about having their writers pinched.

And so acute is the writer shortage that script fees have risen dramatically, with *Hollyoaks* paying around £6,000 for a single script, and experienced writers on *The Bill* being paid around £17,000.

There are simply not enough skilled writers to go round. Every year, as the big drama series limber up for production, script editors are stressed, shouted at, and not infrequently sacked, because they cannot find enough skilled writing talent to script their programmes. It is the same story in comedy. Every year the BBC and Channel 4 actively seek out new writers in the hope of finding the next *Green Wing* or *The Office*.

SKILLS AND TECHNIQUES

The first truth, of course, is that writing any kind of drama – theatre, radio, or television – is a skilled craft. It is something that can encompass genius. It is what Shakespeare did, and Ben Jonson, and Moliere and Sheridan. It is an activity that requires not only facility with words and skill with structure, but an acute sensitivity regarding people and the way they behave.

A dramatist is an architect, who uses words and pictures instead of bricks and girders to construct an edifice in which every word has its proper place and serves its proper function. To do this skilfully requires techniques and disciplines that no new writer can be expected to know intuitively. Yet out of the 10,000 scripts sent to the BBC each year, only a minority show evidence that the writer has made any attempt at all to study the craft of scriptwriting.

WHAT THE AUDIENCE WANTS

A second truth is that television drama demands more of its writers than most other mediums. Every writer of fiction, be it books, stage plays, or broadcast, is a storyteller, a weaver of tales. But television dramatists must do more than captivate an audience: they must captivate a *mass* audience. If you write a novel that explores the theological choices facing Chilean monks in the early 19th century you might, with luck, find a publisher somewhere willing to print a few copies. If your subject is utterly incomprehensible you might even win a major literary prize.

But this won't do for television. Television – on whatever level – is about entertainment. It may be entertainment of high ambition and cultural value (consider the small but admirable drama output of BBC4) or entertainment that seeks only to please for a fleeting moment. But every television drama – however literary or demanding its subject – must aim to satisfy millions of people. 'Drama draws people together with its powerful emotions and irresistible storytelling', says the BBC. For any writer, let alone one inexperienced and new to the media, the task of attracting and holding so wide an audience must be daunting.

HIGH COST = HIGH RISK

The high cost of television drama is another factor working against the new, inexperienced writer. Major BBC film drama 'events' (these days often shown over two nights) can cost up to two million pounds to make. An episode of a series like *Silent Witness* or *Robin Hood* will cost anything between £500,000 ('low' price band drama) and £900,000 ('high' price band drama). Even the cost of a half-hour episode of a low-budget soap opera is well over £100,000. An editor has to be very brave to commission an inexperienced writer, however promising, to script a production that is going to cost half-a-million pounds. Inevitably the editor must ask:

- Will the new writer be able to cope with technical problems?

- Will they be able to act on the notes they are given for a second, or third draft?

- Will they become difficult and emotional when script changes urged by the editor and producer are criticised by the executive producer who demands another huge rewrite?

- Will they be able to come up with further rewrites half-way through shooting when the actor playing the lead has been admitted, overnight, to a clinic for alcoholics?

Huge amounts of money are at stake! The competitive edge of the channel against the opposition is at stake! More importantly, the script editor's job is at stake! The temptation is to go with the tried-and-trusted writer. He might be burnt-out and weary unto death, but he will at least deliver a script that is the right length, with the right number of characters, and the right number of scenes.

WORKING IN YOUR FAVOUR

Despite the obstacles, the opportunities are there waiting to be taken. Look at the factors operating in your favour:

- Television drama and situation comedy is a rapidly expanding market.

- Script editors are expected to find new writers. If they fail they risk being sacked. They are as eager to find you as you are to find them.

- Just one programme, the BBC's *Doctors*, will use up to 30 totally new writers in a series.

- Because there is no formal scriptwriter qualification, no 'script school' or college, all new writers start on the outside, and come from diverse and often unlikely backgrounds. A shop assistant in Barrow-in-Furness is just as likely to succeed as a film school graduate in London.

- Comedy writers are in such demand that the BBC runs regular scriptwriting competitions, with script development help and workshops. Channel 4's website *4laughs* is designed to nurture up-and-coming comedy talent discovered through the site.

- The turn-over in existing writers is high. Apart from the normal loss due to age and mortality, television scriptwriters frequently turn to other areas of writing – novels, stage plays – or start up independent production companies and become producers. Others, sadly, find that their scripts are no longer the kind that is wanted.

- Most scripts by new writers are very poor. They are often hand-written, the dialogue dull, the stories repetitive and the plotting obvious. Spelling can be atrocious, and layout careless, with many crossings-out. The urge to write television drama is at its strongest amongst the socially maladjusted – people who cannot cope very well with real life, and seek to live through a fantasy world of their own making. Semi-literates send in scripts – and all too often, the cynic might say, they are accepted. Ninety-per-cent of scripts can be – and are – mentally dismissed after reading half a page.

♦ Few new writers know the type of script they should be writing, or even what to do with their script when they have written it.

HOW TO SUCCEED

In the first place you must write a script that you can show as an example of your writing skills. This script may never be made into a programme – but that doesn't matter, even though it is made with blood, sweat, and tears, and is the joy and pride of your life. This script is your CV. It is known in various script units as a 'calling card' script. Its purpose is to show script editors, agents, and producers, that you have the talent to write dialogue, invent characters, and construct stories. You might be lucky and sell it for production, but it will have done its job brilliantly if it gets you a commission to write an episode of a series drama like *Where the Heart Is,* or a soap like *Emmerdale,* or an invitation to join a sitcom workshop.

To impress and excite your script must be:

♦ original in concept
♦ well constructed
♦ confidently plotted
♦ have good dialogue
♦ have good characterisation
♦ be professionally presented.

In the second place you must learn how to sell your script – and thus sell yourself as a writer. To do this you will need to know:

- the kind of drama that television script editors are looking for

- the programmes that are actively looking for new writers

- how to get your script read by the only people that matter: those with the power to commission you to write.

This book is designed to help you to achieve all of these aims. Its first part gives you professional hints on how to write your script – tips that producers, agents, and script editors would give you themselves if they had the time. Its second part gives you the vital inside information you need to actually sell yourself as a writer.

THE REWARDS

In the coming months there will be many, many writers who receive rejection letters. But somewhere there will be a writer – perhaps on the point of giving up hope – who answers the phone one dull, dreary morning and finds himself or herself being told something on the lines of: 'Brilliant script! We're going ahead with it straight away. Contracts department will be on to you about the fee. Can we have lunch tomorrow to talk about casting? We thought of Keira Knightly for the main role, but we'd like your opinion so I've asked her to lunch as well.'

Perhaps that writer will be you.

'There are two struggles: the struggle to write something good and the struggle to get it read. You have to attack both with single-minded persistence.'

(Christopher McQuarrie, writer of *The Usual Suspects*)

$$\left(1 \right)$$

The Basics

THE CALLING CARD SCRIPT

You are going to write a 'calling card' television script
that will show your talents as a writer. This script is
terribly important: in fact, it's the only thing that is
important. Nobody in television will care about what
you've done in life, or who you are, or who you know, or
what your thoughts are about *Eastenders* plotlines these
days. All anybody will care about is:

a) can you write?
b) can you write the sort of script I'm looking for?

Your 'calling card' script, as it is known in most script
units, is expected to show what you can produce using
your own skills, imagination, and judgement. It is the *play
that you yourself want to write* and it will respected as
such. That said, and without compromising the script you
believe will do justice to your talents, it makes sense to
target the market that you ultimately want to write for.

Perhaps you already have a story in your head – some
characters – a subject you believe will make a great
drama. But how do you know if it is the right sort of script
to 'sell' you as a writer? Or how many characters and
locations you ought to have? Or how long it ought to be?
Before we consider anything else, let us look at the basics:

- the best length at which to write
- the ideal number of characters and locations
- the best kind of drama to write.

THE BEST LENGTH AT WHICH TO WRITE

Recognised writing slots are:

- 90-minutes for major 'event' drama. The advantage of writing a major 90-minute play is that it shows your ability to create characters, to write dialogue, to utilise the camera, and to handle your plot. It also shows that you are capable of sustained writing on a major theme. Major 'event' dramas can be longer than 90-minutes – they can be a two-parter, spread over two consecutive nights' viewing, but it is pointless for a new writer to attempt anything longer than a 90-minute script.

- 60-minutes for series and serial drama. The advantage of the 60-minute play is that it shows the above virtues without requiring script editors to read as much. It also saves you printing and postage costs. And if you are writing to a common theme – e.g. love lost/found/ betrayed or the paranormal – it has a faint (but real) chance of being 'packaged' with others in a season of one-hour themed stories.

- 30-minutes for soap operas and sitcoms. This is not a good length for a calling card drama script. To open, develop, and conclude an original drama in 30 minutes is very difficult. Other than *Doctors* there are rarely any 30-minute slots for self-contained dramas, and soaps are not interested in reading scripts written for their existing characters/plots. If you are interested in writing a sitcom, however, this is the length to aim for.

◆ 10-minutes for drama 'shorts'. The advantage of writing a 10-minute short is that it is short – and the script editor is therefore more likely to actually read it. It gives a glimpse of your talents without requiring labour and effort. 10-minute shorts are, though, at the end of the day less convincing than a solid 90 or 60-minute play, they are very difficult to write, and there may not be any 10-minute series in production (and consequently no script editor to read your effort).

THE IDEAL NUMBER OF CHARACTERS AND LOCATIONS

A new writer will generally find it easier to introduce and develop a small group of characters, rather than juggle with a large cast, and it is certainly a kindness to the script reader who is now reading her fourth or fourteenth script of the day. It is also wise for the new writer not to get entangled in location action that involves complex camerawork. That said, there is virtually no market today for plays that involve very few people sitting in a room talking to each other. Today's television audience is blasé and easily bored. Producers who want high viewing figures (i.e. all of them) must try to provide the sort of action and location-shooting common to the cinema and to films made for the video market. Your script (unless it is a sitcom, see chapter 9) needs to take us out and about, and include visual action. You also stand more chance of success if you give good 'production values' (i.e. provide interesting things to look at) at a relatively low cost. From a budget point of view, a play that has only half-a-dozen principal characters, and takes advantage of, say, the scenic beauty of a nature reserve, a fairground, or perhaps the haunting, sad atmosphere of a seaside resort in winter, is good. A play that requires a cast of thousands, location shooting in Paraguay, and a comet crashing on the Houses of Parliament, is bad. It is true that major drama 'events' have multi-million pound feature-film budgets and can afford global locations, special effects, and large casts, but these films and series are invariably written by experienced writers.

THE BEST KIND OF DRAMA TO WRITE

Some types of drama are more in demand that others. Some are to be avoided by a new writer. Here we look at:

♦ socially-aware drama
♦ human-relationship drama
♦ historical drama
♦ sci-fi and the paranormal
♦ existing series and serials
♦ children's drama
♦ adaptations
♦ comedy drama
♦ situation comedy.

Socially-aware drama

The BBC and Channel 4 have traditionally been proud of their reputation for tough, contemporary, socially-aware drama, and there was a time when most one-off television plays had something to tell us about society in Britain. The years of *The Wednesday Play* and *Play for Today* are gone, but a contemporary drama dealing with social

Our drama series need to feel smart and stylish and relevant to the lives and loves of a 25–34 year old drama audience – 75% of whom have young families and all are asking questions and exploring all areas of adult life.

BBC 3 commissioning brief

issues (e.g. Channel 4's major 2007 two-parter *Britz* about young Muslims living under Britain's anti-terrorist laws) is, nevertheless, your safest bet. Even if your play is not bought, it will most clearly show your ability to write contemporary dialogue and characterisation. '*Eastenders, Holby City* and *Casualty* will continue to tackle difficult and sensitive issues' says BBC 1. In truth, socially-aware drama does not have to be relentlessly grim and serious: many are written as love stories, comedies (see below), or as thrillers that take us into the world of high finance or environmental disaster. Can you find an area of modern life that has not been exploited by others? Is there something about which you feel strongly? Something you passionately want to write about?

Human relationship drama

You will not go far wrong – in terms of subject matter – if you write a story of human relationships: a story of romance, love, sex, and possibly intrigue and

'The trick is to have a really good story and really good characters.'

Writer Lucy Gannon, *On Air*, BBC2

betrayal. And if you set it against a background of contemporary life and involve contemporary social issues, your subject matter will have even greater appeal, because you will be combining what the viewers want to see with what the producers and directors want to do. Such a script will show your potential to write for a wide range of soap operas and series dramas. Just as plays about social issues do not have to be relentlessly grim, stories about love do not need to be soft and romantic. Plays in the strand *Love Bites* included a tale of single parents and drug addicts in Glasgow; a searing study of date rape (which included flash-forwards and split screens); and a bitter-sweet comedy about love between a black girl and a white boy.

Historical drama

Avoid unless you have a stunning idea that the programmers cannot resist. Certainly the market is growing, particularly for dramatisations of events in the recent past (e.g. *The Lavender List* about the last days of the Wilson government and BBC2's hugely ambitious *Decades*), and popular series like *Robin Hood* and *Hornblower* have been very successful. But the expense is great, most historical plays that reach the screen are adaptations (see below), and projects generally originate with programme makers rather than writers. Another problem is that agents and script editors have difficulty assessing your skill with modern dialogue and characterisation when you are writing in a period setting.

Sci Fi and the paranormal

Very much in vogue, from a rejuvenated *Dr Who* and its spin off *Torchwood* to *Afterlife* and *Sea of Souls*. Subjects and settings can be diverse: BBC 1's *Empathy* follows an ex-con whose paranormal visions assist in a murder hunt; *Lifeline* is a supernatural love story. *Life on Mars* carries us back in time, while ITV's more scientifically credible *Time of Your Life* is about a 36-year-old who wakes up from a coma after 19 years. If you have a good idea, go for it.

Existing soaps and series

Do not write a script for an existing programme like *Coronation Street,* or *The Bill,* even if you eventually want to write for the programme concerned. Most script editors will not even look at your script – they are interested in your own original talent, not in how well you copy what you see on the screen.

Serials

Most serials are written by one writer. If you have a cracking story that you believe needs telling over several episodes you should write the first episode (60 minutes) and short summaries of the other episodes. Even if the series is not made, it will show your dramatic skills and creativity.

Children's drama

There's quite a lot of it, but the market for new writers is not as great as that for adult series and soaps. If this is your interest, your best bet is to devise a four-part or six-part serial, and write one episode together with synopses of the rest. It might not be accepted, but if your work is liked you will be encouraged and pointed in the direction of children's programmes that use outside writers. Children's drama is almost always low-budget.

Adaptations

Although adaptations – particularly of classic novels or detective stories – are frequently made there is no opportunity here for the new writer.

Comedy drama

Very much in demand, but surprisingly little reaches the screen. *The Beiderbecke Affair* is the classic serial, *Auf Wiedersehen Pet* so popular it was revived. ITV's single plays are often comedy drama. Writing realistic drama that also makes us laugh is not easy, but if your instincts take you in this direction there is a ready market.

Situation comedy

This is a big market, and both the BBC, Channel 4 and ITV are actively looking for new writing talent. See chapter 9 for specific sitcom writing requirements, and chapter 13 for information about what programme makers want.

COMMON QUERIES

Is it true that anyone of average ability can learn how to be a scriptwriter?
You must have an aptitude for writing dialogue. Everything else can be learned.

Is it true that you should always write about what you know about?
Generally speaking, yes. But you need to avoid the more obvious situations. Producers get sent a lot of dramas about students living in squalid flats from students living in squalid flats, and about teachers who are sick and tired of teaching from teachers who are sick and tired of teaching. That said, a doctor, nurse, or hospital porter is more likely to write a hospital drama with conviction than is a solicitor. Script editors are impressed – or at the simplest level comforted – if they believe you are writing

with inside knowledge. This does not mean that you can't write a drama about life on Mars unless you've been there; it does mean that you need to know everything there is to know about Mars and the technology needed to sustain life on it.

The setting and subject do not have to be exotic. Stacking supermarket shelves at night might not be glamorous and exciting, but if your story is well told viewers will be fascinated to know the hidden dramas, rivalries, loves, and routines of supermarket life in the secret hours of the night.

BBC Two drama aims to ring true with the big themes in the life of the diverse UK audience. We deliver this through our commitment to the best writing and on screen talent.

BBC 2 statement of programme policy

How gritty and controversial can I be?
As gritty and controversial as you like. Putting on gritty controversial plays makes BBC and Channel 4 producers feel that they are more than mere hacks in the entertainment business: it makes them feel that they are people of influence in society. In recent years we have seen television dramas about drugs abuse, child abuse, incest, oppression within the family, homosexual oppression, rent boys, transvestites, lesbians, racial tension, prison scandals, mob violence, and corruption. Studies in fidelity, honesty, loyalty, and the happy state of England, however, are only seen on ITV.

So aren't gritty, controversial plays old hat?
Well, possibly. Today's drama heads and commissioning editors are likely to be more concerned with property values in the Ardeche than social values in inner-city Britain, and today's script editors (who are nearly all in their twenties) seem to be apolitical, though healthily interested in sex and money. A play about old-age pensioners dying of hypothermia might make their eyes glaze over, but give them a script called *Lesbian Snogs* and they'll sit up and take an interest right away.

The truth is that they want it all. 'BBC Two drama offers thought-provoking storytelling,' says the BBC. 'We are more than ever committed to drama as entertainment,' says Channel 4.

So make your play thought-provoking *and* entertaining, and everybody will like it

Are some subjects or settings more likely to be accepted than others?
Yes, but fashions can change very quickly, and all script editors are liable to decide they're sick of buggery plays just as you put the finishing touches to a cracking 90-minutes on the subject. There might be a leaning towards northern drama series (a successful heart-warming family saga set in the North will be followed by two or three others in similar locations), or there might be a fashion for witty, ironic plays set among young people in London, but by the time you catch the mood of the moment it will have changed, and although it only takes a second on your computer to change 'Iona' to 'Islington' throughout

your script, it is unlikely to help you sell it. By the time a drama reaches the screen it might well be three years on from the time when it was proposed, and two years, perhaps, from the time when it was commissioned.

'Any series should be based around a bold, provocative idea, covering worlds you have not seen before or from a fresh angle... the target demographic is 16 to 34, but we do not want to make that too exclusive.'

Ben Stephenson, Channel 4 Drama

Both Channel 4 and BBC 3 very clearly and openly target younger audiences (after you're 35 you might as well be dead).

The constants, of course, on all channels, are police/detective dramas and medical dramas. Or dramas that cleverly combine both elements.

Is it all right to use 'bad' language if it's realistic and true to character?
In moderation, but a surprisingly high percentage of scripts from new writers have characters using crude language, repetitiously, and this doesn't impress script editors, because they are professionals looking for scripts that can be broadcast. (See chapter 7).

What if I have a great idea for a series of 30-minute dramas, and don't think the stories will stretch to an hour?
Write to the length you are comfortable with. Script editors would much rather read a good 30-minute script, even if

they don't have any 30-minute slots available, than a 60-minute script that rambles about. And there is always the possibility of a 30-minute drama strand being launched in the future (particularly in a low-budget, late night slot).

Are any drama slots specifically designed for new writing talent?
The BBC provides opportunities for new writers through low-cost drama series like *Doctors* and has an excellent website (*www.bbc.co.uk/writersroom*) devoted to seeking and nurturing new writing talent. The Writersroom also produces an information pack which gives advice on possible markets, current trends in drama, and script opportunities (see chapter 19). Another good source of information about new writing slots, and indeed about much else, is the bi-monthly Scriptwriter Magazine (*www. scriptwritermagazine.com*). Much of the search for new comedy writing is now done online (a good source of information and advice is Robin Kelly's Writing for Performance, *www.writing.org.uk*). If Channel 4 has a new comedy writer slot it will give details on its website (*www.channel4. com/4laughs*). For more detailed advice see chapter 18.

Should my script for the BBC be longer than for ITV or Channel 4, because there will be no advertising breaks?
Nobody is going to be timing your calling card script, and it wouldn't matter if they did, because the BBC makes many programmes to the same length as the commercial channels in order to allow for advertising breaks if they are sold abroad. (This also has the happy effect of allowing the BBC promotions department several minutes every hour to fill with programme trails).

Should I put commercial breaks in my calling card script?
Yes, in the version you send to ITV or Channel 4 or
Channel 5. Not in the version you send to the BBC. You
should not call them commercial breaks, but 'End of Part
One' 'End of Part Two' etc.

SUMMARY

- ◆ 60-minutes is a good length for an original calling-card
  drama script and 30-minutes for a sitcom. Don't
  worry about accurate timing, but using a standard
  layout (see chapter 10) your drama script should be
  around 60 pages long, and your sitcom around 40
  pages long, depending on just how fast and funny it is.

- ◆ You should write a contemporary play, because this
  will more easily demonstrate your ability with
  dialogue and characterisation.

- ◆ It is better to introduce and develop a small group of
  characters than to juggle with a large cast. The critical
  part of your calling card script is the first 10 pages. If
  you succeed in writing even one interesting character,
  in an interesting situation, and *leave the script editor
  wanting to know more*, you will have done very well.

- ◆ You should give us visual interest (without demanding
  enormous special effects) and show that you can cut
  between interior and exterior scenes.

- ◆ It will be an added bonus if you can give us an insight
  into an area of life we would not otherwise know about.

The BBC advises new writers to write the sort of play they
themselves would like to see on the screen, choosing
subjects from their own experience.

$$\left(\!\!\begin{array}{c}2\end{array}\!\!\right)$$

Story and Theme

This chapter, and the following chapters on style, structure, plotting, visual interest, dialogue, and characterisation, are designed to stimulate your creativity and help you to avoid common errors when writing your 'calling-card' script. Here we look at the difference between your superficial story and the underlying subject matter.

WHAT IS YOUR PLAY *REALLY* ABOUT?

You have decided on:

- the length of script you are going to write
- the story you are going to tell.

But what is the subject of your drama? Will it be about love – love betrayed, love that endures? Or about passion – passion that triumphs over all odds, passion that betrays and destroys? Or will it perhaps be about social justice – justice that triumphs, justice that is blind, justice that is abused?

The underlying subject of a play is sometimes known as **'the theme'** or **'the premise'**. It's what your play is about on a deeper level than the actual story. If an Elizabethan script editor had been asked to sum up *Othello* he might well have said: 'Jealousy.' Or he might have expanded slightly and said: 'The study of a man destroyed by his own unreasoned jealousy.' Alan Plater's play *Belonging*, transmitted on ITV 1 in 2004, was a play about a woman whose life was turned upside-down when her dependable husband disappeared, leaving her to care for his three elderly relatives. But it was also, said critic Stephen Pile, 'a moving meditation on selfishness, service and freedom.' Single plays – particularly those of 60-minute or 90-minute duration – need to contain thoughts and ideas over and above the bricks and mortar of the actual story they tell. Producers and script editors know that *Othello* is more than a bit of chicanery that leads to a nasty domestic crisis. When they read your script they need to be convinced that your play has something to tell us about human nature or about contemporary life.

'A theme is an idea ... about life and its meaning, about the human condition. It is the underlying truth signified by the film — universal, enduring, significant, expressive and eloquent. It springs from the writer's view of the way the world is and his sense of morality of the way the world should be.'

William Miller, American writer and film maker

Consider the following story idea:

SAMMY SLIME is manager of the Hardtimes Residential Home for the Elderly. It is a council home but because of the 'privatisation' of social service inspectorate staff (recently and controversially introduced, perhaps, in the real world) he finds that he can claim state money for his residents without accounting for expenditure. Slowly he starves the residents, depriving them of food and heating and comfort until there is a dreary, debilitating reign of terror.

ELSIE, a courageous woman in her nineties, tries to rally opposition to SLIME. But she is frail and catches pneumonia. We know that she will soon die unless SLIME is exposed.

The social services – council workers, overworked doctors – all fail to spot what is happening.

The other old folk long to help ELSIE – but are terrified of SLIME. Surely they will be shamed into helping her? They almost mount a rebellion – but not quite.

ELSIE's daughter is due from America. Will she turn up in time?

She doesn't. ELSIE dies. SLIME covers up evidence of malnutrition and gets a death certificate from a harassed young GP.

It seems that he can get away with everything. Until a dustman finds three dozen empty catfood tins outside the back door...

And the local papers get hold of the story, and investigate.

Shorn of names like Slime and Hardtimes, used here to avoid libel risks inherent in realistic names (see **libel**, page 208) this is a sound enough, if rather gloomy narrative that would once have had considerable appeal to the BBC or Channel 4. In it we see a man in power ill-treating victims in his care. We see a victim try to oppose him. We wait for the social services or doctors to help the victim – and are horrified when they fail. We see a sudden ray of hope when the daughter is due from America! We see the hope dashed – and the victim die. We then see retribution come from an unexpected but logical quarter.

This is the narrative – the superficial story. But it does not tell us how the play will actually be written, or what the play is actually about.

ANALYSING THE STORY OUTLINE

◆ Is it the story of Elsie, a woman who has perhaps been too timid during her life but who finds, when she is in her nineties, the strength to lead a struggle against oppression?

The play will thus be a story of courage in extremity, and the triumph of the human spirit.

◆ Is it the story of Sammy Slime? Perhaps as a young man Sam went into his career with high ideals and a genuine desire to help his fellow human beings. Perhaps he makes his first 'profit' by mistake ... then when he is not discovered, and when the old people do not notice, he is tempted to take a 'profit' yet again.

The play will thus be a study of how avarice consumes and destroys a man.

◆ Is it the story of the social services, underfunded for decades, with doctors that cannot cope, now inflicted with a form of 'privatisation' that leaves the people it ought to protect exposed to sordid profiteers?

Thus it will be a highly partisan political play, a trumpet call to the government to reverse its policies.

The dramatist might say he wants to combine all these elements. The theme or premise might be: 'A searing exposure of neglect in our society, told through the battle of wills between a woman who finds courage she did not know she possessed, and a weak man who falls to temptation.'

Understanding your subject helps you to write your play. Even working it out in your head encourages you to probe deeper into your characters' minds, and understand their motivations. You must always know what you are writing about.

THE DANGERS OF TOO MUCH ANALYSIS

At the same time you have to be careful of this sort of analysis. You can dignify anything if you try hard enough, and the tale of Slime and Elsie (the story of a woman of deep strength and a man of moral weakness) is already sounding like a textual analysis of Macbeth. In his book *The Way to*

'If you want to send a message, use Western Union.'

(Hollywood producer)

Write for Television Eric Paice points out that you can make *Little Red Riding Hood* mean anything from 'Wolves should make sure there are no woodcutters around before they dress up in drag' to 'Little girls should have their eyes tested before visiting their grandmothers.'

But a good play, whether it deals with contemporary social issues or not, should always operate on two levels: the story and the idea behind the story. Writing must go deep, and find, beneath the narrative, a thought that will illuminate our view of the world.

SUMMARY

◆ Be clear about the underlying theme of your play – the issues it raises, the emotions it explores. This will make it easier to plot your story, develop your characters, and reach an effective and powerful conclusion.

$$\bigodot_{3}$$

Style

WHAT TYPE OF PLAY ARE YOU WRITING?

You know your story, and your characters. You have considered the **theme** of your play – its message, the issues it deals with.

But what **style** should you write in? Will you write a straightforward, realistic, documentary-type of play, with the camera used as an unseen eye to record the scene? Or will you include elements of artifice – people speaking to camera, special effects, flash-backs, fantasy? As the play's narrator, will you allow viewers to know everything that is happening, or will you deliberately keep your audience in the dark about some aspects of the story to encourage their curiosity?

You might call a play 'a love story', but what kind of love story? You may decide to write a comedy, but is it:

- A social comedy, employing wit and irony?
- A farce?
- A black comedy?
- A savage satire?

Viewers will be confused (before them, of course, and more importantly, script readers will be confused) if a much-loved character suddenly develops cancer in the middle of a frothy farce, or if an exposé of homelessness in London is suddenly over-run with bikini-clad girls hiding in wardrobes.

You might argue that drama needs to tear itself free of conventions (Dennis Potter's drama did), but to break the conventions you need first to understand them and to have the ability to write within them. At the very least, you must be breaking them deliberately.

In this chapter we look at:

- plays that show the world as it is (called **narrative realism**)
- plays that utilize fantasy and the imagination (**non-realism**)
- ways to tell your story
- ways in which the camera can tell your story.

NARRATIVE REALISM

In narrative realism we are out there in real life, in the world of drizzly afternoons, Job Centres and super-markets. The locations are real, the characters are credible, the stories believable. *Cathy Come Come* is the benchmark, a play that looked back to films like *Saturday Night and Sunday Morning* and *Room at the Top*. Critics say narrative realism is boring and pedestrian, doing something that ought to be done by the straightforward television documentary, and failing to use properly the possibilities of television. Nevertheless, this type of play has many defenders, and is the most accessible form of drama for the new writer. In recent years it has gained a

new and controversial lease of life through the drama-
documentary – fiction based on real events. Narrative
realism plays are invariably filmed on location rather than
in the studio. In narrative realism you should maintain the
following conventions:

- **Surface accuracy**. In simple terms this means that a
  fireman's uniform should be a real fireman's uniform.
  People who ask for drinks in pubs should have to pay
  for them – and if the price is mentioned it should be
  believable. The law of the land, as it exists in your
  script, should conform to the law as we understand it
  in the real world. If the main character in your crime
  thriller is a school headmistress, and you find that you
  want her to interrogate suspects (something that
  school headmistresses do not do), you must not let
  her do it without providing a logical, believable excuse.

- **Cause and effect**. At its simplest, if somebody is lying in
  the garden in a swimsuit we should expect it to be
  summer and the sun shining. If a woman punches a
  man violently in a restaurant other diners should
  respond in a believable manner. (This will depend, of
  course, on where the event is taking place: Cheltenham
  diners might be expected to respond differently from
  diners in Rome.)

- **Psychological consistency**. If a character is sensible,
  they should remain sensible *unless their change in
  character is part of your story*. If a character suddenly
  stops being good-natured and becomes spiteful, viewers will try to find a reason, and puzzle over how it fits
  into the story you are telling.

- **Normal expectations of character and behaviour.** What is portrayed should conform to a common-sense view of what happens in the world. In some ways this is a dodgy rule, a great worry to the politically correct. It means that if the camera strays into a household of Asian immigrants we should expect to find a curry on the table. In the country mansion of Sir Roddy Forescue Bart, we should expect to find roast beef. Reverse the menus without explanation, and viewers will be confused. They will fret over why Sir Roddy is munching curry and the immigrants passing the mustard.

This is a perfectly valid rule, but it does inevitably reinforce stereotypes, and it can make scripts dull and predictable. The writer should try to present a view of the world that is credible but at the same time fresh and different, which is, of course, easier said than done.

NON-REALISTIC DRAMA

This can be simply heightened drama – the characters deliberately larger than life, as seen in many comedies – or it can move into fantasy and use the camera to show us images, ideas, thoughts that might be in the characters' heads. Some dramas combine realism with fantasy, notable examples being *Selling Hitler* and before that *Wingate* and David Rudkin's *Penda's Fen*. In *Trainspotting* the addict swims down the lavatory bowl seeking his lost drugs. Among modern television dramatists Dennis Potter was the most distinguished in carrying the torch for drama of the imagination. In 2004, BBC 1 acknowledged its debt to Potter with its serial *Blackpool*.

The new writer is often tempted to write fantasy. It frees him from the tedious constraint of believable characterization, logical plots and credible dialogue. But only the most skilled and confident – not to say established – writer can normally break conventions with impunity, and until he is in a position to explain his idea to Channel 4's Head of Drama over lunch, the new writer should stick to the grim business of devising stories that we can believe in.

On the other hand, a major new talent that is exciting and different and revolutionary in its use of the medium, must make – and break – the rules.

WAYS TO TELL YOUR STORY

The way you tell (**narrate**) your story depends on how best you think you can grip your audience and hold its interest.

The omniscient narrator

The narrator knows more than the characters, and lets viewers share the knowledge. In a crime story we see the murder committed. We know the identity of the murderer. We watch the detective stumbling – with many a false trail – towards the truth. This technique can give a valuable element of suspense (will the villain be caught or will the nice chap who has been framed get sent down for ten years by which time his poor widowed Mum will be dead?) but you lose the element of mystery.

The narrator as character

Sometimes the narrator knows only what the principal character knows. We unravel the mystery with the detective, sharing his or her thoughts. This is straight realism, the classic whodunnit.

The narrator as a tease

Sometimes the narrator pretends to know only what the principal characters know, but occasionally reveals other things to us. (Miss Brown stops sobbing and smiles bravely. Detective Inspector Boot takes back his hankie and leaves the room. Miss Brown's expression changes. She picks up the letter. She stares at it, her expression cold. She suddenly rips it into pieces. CUT to the next scene.) Here we cannot be certain that it was Miss Brown whodidit, but we know she is not what she seems – and we thus know more than the detective. This is a very dangerous technique, for if the camera can tell us a bit about what's happening, why can't it tell us everything?

The narrator in the dark

Sometimes the narrator knows less than the characters. Detective Inspector Boot says: 'So that is how he did it – no, don't ask me to tell you, not until my final experiment, but arrange for Madam de Courville and the ticket inspector to be entering this building at precisely 7pm.' This was the basis of the Sherlock Holmes stories, of course. In lesser hands it is a technique that can be infuriating. If Boot knows who did it why doesn't he tell us instead of being smug?

The cheating narrator

The viewer will rapidly, if unconsciously, know which technique you are employing and will expect you to stick to it. If we are solving the crime in company with the detective and suddenly (tempted by the need for a dramatic moment) you show us, the viewers, something that the detective does not know, the play will be in danger of losing dramatic tension.

The real narrator

To make a great movie, you need just three things: a great script, a great script, and a great script.

(Alfred Hitchcock)

The real narrator, of course, knows everything. The real narrator (you the writer) has decided which dramatic technique to use.

WAYS THE CAMERA CAN NARRATE YOUR STORY

This is a topic that can get fairly esoteric, and is much debated by media course lecturers (is the camera being used in the mode of *histoire* or *discours?*). New writers should avoid getting bogged down in such questions. At its simplest there are two basic narrative modes:

The impartial narrator

The camera has no viewpoint (although clearly somebody has selected the images and words). We see a succession of things happen as recorded by an impartial eye.

The active narrator

The camera overtly presents us with opinions on what is happening, or on the views that are being expressed (the camera pans along a wall of china ducks while a character is heard saying, 'I've always prided myself on my good taste'); or a character glances to camera and winks as Francis Urquhart did in *House of Cards* or speaks directly to camera (see the opening of Sharon Foster's *Shoot the Messenger* in the BBC Writersroom online script archive).

SUMMARY

◆ Most writers use straightforward narrative realism but also employ the camera actively to point up mood, give pace, and emphasise characterisation. (See Chapter 6, Visual Interest.) This is an effective method and shows agents and editors that you can think visually and use the camera.

♦ Don't get bogged down worrying about who the narrator is. You will almost certainly get it right by instinct. Refer back to this chapter, though, if you get into trouble.

4

Structure

SIMPLER THAN IT LOOKS

Entire books are written about structure. There are those who believe in surface structure and deep structure, who can plot structure on a graph, who can tell you what to do between pages 1 and 5 and between pages 5 and 10 and so on. All this is useful and interesting for students of critical analysis but it can stifle the talents of a writer. Shakespeare, we can be confident, did not have little graphs of character development (set-up and focus point), story development (conflict and confrontation) and climax (moment of truth) on his desk when he penned *King Lear*.

If you take account of the following points you will get your structure right instinctively, without having your freedom to write as your imagination takes you unnecessarily constrained:

- the basic structure
- the opening
- classic hooks to keep viewers watching
- structuring for commercial breaks
- multi-strand structuring.

THE BASIC STRUCTURE

This is the broad shape of any play. Keep to it and you will not go far wrong.

1. **Situation.** You present us with a visual setting, the main characters, and the beginning of a story that interests us and makes us want to go on watching. This invariably involves conflict of some kind (see **conflict in drama**, page 45).

2. **Complication.** The situation you set up in the beginning needs to be complicated, false trails need to be laid, the aims and ambitions of your characters frustrated. At the same time we must be clear about where we are heading, and our interest must not wane.

3. **Reversal.** If things went badly for your hero they should now change and start to go better. Conversely, if your hero has been doing well, things should now go badly (**retardation** of the story).

4. **Climax.** The central issue of your drama must come to a climax – the conflict come to a head. This can be done through dialogue or through action on the screen. As this is television, a visual climax is preferred. In series drama it is traditionally 'the car chase'. The car chase need not involve cars – it can be a gunman pursuing another through an empty warehouse, or anything else that involves action, movement and pace.

5. **Resolution.** Something must have changed. It may be a

purely physical resolution (your hero and heroine united; your villain dragged off to gaol) or it may be an alteration in your characters' attitude to life, towards each other. Perhaps your **twist resolution** is that they are not changed at all. If aliens seize a gardener from his allotment and require him to undergo unbelievable terrors in order to save the galaxy – and the last thing we see is him back in his vegetable plot checking his potatoes and muttering 'The things you have to do in this life, I don't know...' – well, that is a resolution in itself.

Another way of putting it is to say that, however disguised, all plays need to have a beginning, a middle, and an end!

THE OPENING

The first 60 seconds are crucially important. The remote control unit has taught producers that viewers are fickle and disloyal. If they are not hooked in the first minute they are liable to press the button and 'zap' to another channel. One writer, chided by a script editor for having a slow opening, replied: 'I did it deliberately! It's to hook the people who have zapped over after the first minute on something else' – but this cunning excuse is unlikely to be accepted. A strong opening is particularly important for mystery or thriller drama series – *Spooks, Midsomer Murders* – where episodes can cost anything up to a million pounds to make, and are designed to anchor the evening's audience to a particular channel and build audiences for future episodes. The way to a good opening is to devise a good hook.

CLASSIC HOOKS TO KEEP VIEWERS WATCHING

Three classic hooks are:

◆ curiosity
◆ mystery
◆ suspense.

Curiosity

Curiosity is the basis of all story-telling. If humans were not intractably curious, if they did not by their very nature always want to know *what will happen next*, then novelists and dramatists would have a lean time of it.

> A woman rushes up to a man and says: 'Well, did you do it?' and he looks at her stony-faced, and then nods, and she says: 'O my God.' End of scene. Opening titles.

Hopefully, we are curious to know what the man has done. Murdered his wife? Had the cat put down? Left the bathroom tap running with disastrous consequences?

> A girl watches through the window as the postman approaches. She is clearly excited. The postman turns in at the gate, and the girl runs through to the hall as an expensive-looking white envelope falls to the mat. She picks it up and turns it over, longing to open it and yet frightened...

There is no mystery yet, because we have not been presented with anything mysterious or odd. But such is the human desire to know what other people are up to, and in particular the desire to see inside other people's letters, that even a mildly curious opening will help to keep viewers hooked.

Mystery

A more powerful hook is the use of mystery. Somebody does something strange, something we cannot account for. A dour, sinister man with a mean, cold face slips into a hotel room with a small plastic device that he furtively places behind a vase of flowers. What is it? A bomb? A microphone?

A man visits a private detective and asks that the Mother Superior of a nunnery should be followed night and day. He will not say why, or give an explanation, but he will pay treble the usual rate. What can she be up to?

Sherlock Holmes stories are built around mysteries; on television *The Avengers* always gave us an opening scene in which something totally odd and unaccountable happened. A huge number of plays and serials depend on the use of mystery to a greater or lesser extent, particularly in the first 60 seconds.

Suspense

Suspense is what keeps us on the edge of our seats. If mystery relies on puzzlement, and not knowing what is going on, suspense is when we know perfectly well what might happen, and are fearful in case it does.

A shadow of a person against a wall in an alleyway, holding a knife. CUT TO: A girl walking along the dark, empty street towards the alley. CUT TO: A police car patrols in a well-lit street nearby. CUT TO: The shadow raises the knife as we hear the girl's footsteps approach. CUT TO: Interior of police car, the driver whistling softly as he turns the car into the dark empty street. CUT TO: The girl reaches the alleyway...

And so on. We are compelled to watch, even if we know that the girl cannot be killed because her engagement to the hero in the next episode is on the cover of *TV Times*.

STRUCTURING FOR COMMERCIAL BREAKS

Like the remote control zapper, commercial breaks give viewers the opportunity to switch to another channel. When structuring a serial or series episode it is vital to lead up to a cliff-hanger before each break. It can involve curiosity, mystery, or suspense. The important thing is that it must make us want to go on watching. When you submit a synopsis or storyline of an episode, the script editor will be looking to see if you have strong commercial breaks.

The one thing you must not do is cheat the viewer. If the dour sinister man with a mean, cold face has slipped furtively into the hotel room, and we have heard edgy ominous music as he carefully placed the plastic device behind the vase of flowers, it is cheating to come back after the commercial break to discover that he is a hotel porter putting air ionisers into the guest rooms.

MULTI-STRAND STRUCTURING

Many plays – and particularly series dramas – have more than one plot. Many have two separate plots and also a comic **sub-plot**. Skilled and experienced writers know how to keep different stories bubbling, but the following tips might be helpful for new writers.

Do not attempt to introduce both stories at once
When you open your play you have to impart a lot of information to the viewers very quickly:

- the visual scene
- the initial characters, their names, backgrounds, the role they have to play
- the initial story
- the 'hook' that will keep people watching.

And you have to do all this in a taut, dramatic and interesting way.

It is hard enough to do this with one major story without confusing the viewer with *two* sets of information.

A good *Boon* episode? – the girl shows her tits and you end up with a car chase.

(Former producer, Central TV's *Boon*)

It makes sense to spend the first half-dozen scenes setting up the first story, take it to a point where it can conveniently rest for a moment (preferably with a good 'hook' to keep people interested), and then turn to story number two.

Try to devise stories that are quite different from each other

This helps with **pace**. A story that needs a lot of explaining, a lot of dialogue, a lot of concentration on what is said, needs to be contrasted with a story that is basically simple and has action.

In the *Boon* episode, *Peacemaker*, examined in Chapter 6, page 52, there are three stories:

1. A pop star due to make his comeback on the Birmingham music scene goes missing. Boon and Margaret have to track him down. This is basically comedy-drama. It is highly visual involving stake-outs and chases through sleazy pubs.

2. A woman wants her husband followed to get proof that he is cheating with his alimony payments. This story is more serious, it is about the consequences of divorce, it has twists as our sympathies are engaged first with one side and then with the other.

3. A comedy sub-story involves Harry entertaining a delegation of Dutch machine tool manufacturers in the Plaza Suite.

In *Peacemaker* the writers are careful to make sure that a comedy-drama sequence from story one is followed by a quieter and more down-to-earth scene from story two; and a scene which imparts a lot of information through dialogue is followed by a scene which is visual.

SUMMARY

♦ In broad terms the first part of your script (25 per cent) should set up the situation: the second part (50 per cent) should complicate or deepen it; the third part (25 per cent) should resolve it. Ignore these proportions, however, if they do not fit your particular story.

♦ Hook the reader on page one by creating curiosity, mystery or suspense.

♦ Always have one of these hooks – curiosity, mystery, suspense – operating on some sort of level.

♦ If you are running two stories, allow the first to be established before introducing the second.

♦ Do not overwhelm viewers with verbal information, particularly in the beginning.

(5)

Plotting

HOW DO YOU MAKE THE PLOT INTERESTING?

You have a story, you have worked out a broad structure, now take a look at how you can write the script in an interesting way. This chapter deals with the following:

- the importance of conflict
- decision-making by principal characters
- consequence of action – cause and effect
- creating sympathy
- plots to avoid.

CONFLICT IN DRAMA

All drama depends on conflict. That is not the same as saying that drama depends on people shouting at each other. Generally speaking, people shouting at each other should be avoided – most people have enough argument in their lives without watching other people bawling their heads off. At its most basic, conflict means that Character A wants something to happen, and Character B wants something different to happen.

This might mean anything from: A murderer wants to escape – a detective wants to arrest him. A schoolmaster wants promotion – another wants to sabotage him. A girl wants a bloke – another girl wants him as well. A girl wants a bloke – another bloke wants the girl. A husband wants bacon for breakfast – his wife wants him to have high-fibre muesli.

What does conflict mean?

It can mean:

♦ a problem to be solved
♦ an obstacle to be overcome
♦ a threat to be handled
♦ a decision to be made
♦ a challenge to be met.

Conflict is not the same as aggression. You could write a 50-minute play based on the conflict between a child who wants a kitten, and her family who don't. You could show her manipulations, her relentless purchase of kitten books, her feverish illness caused by not having a kitten, her letters to Father Christmas, finally her finding (or buying) a kitten and bringing it home and hiding it... and the entire play could be gentle and humorous and non-aggressive.

> There is only one plot in TV drama. There's a guy in Zanzibar with a cork up his arse. The only guy in the world who can get it out lives in Newark, New Jersey. We spend the next 50 minutes watching the second guy fighting overwhelming odds to reach the first guy before he dies of toxic poisoning.
>
> (US film distributor)

What does conflict include?

It can include the following:

Man versus elements

Can the mountaineers reach the top of Everest before the storm descends? Will superb seamanship bring the yacht with a hole in it safe to harbour? Can the cork-extracting man from New Jersey fight his way on foot through the Zanzibar mangrove swamps?

Man versus time

Can the cork-extracting man from New Jersey fight his way through the Zanzibar swamps in time? Can the rescue squad find the boy lost in the potholes before he dies of hunger? Can the hero struggling on foot through the blizzard (man versus elements) reach the girl in the wooden shack before the rapist arrives in his snowmobile?

Man versus himself

Can Sir Thomas More reconcile his conscience to swearing allegiance to Henry VIII as head of the Church? Can the Old Labour MP accept the British Telecom shares left to him by his aunty? Can the student who cheated at her exam accept the prize scholarship, knowing that she is depriving a fellow-student who is desperately hard-up? Can the newly divorced man conquer his overwhelming depression?

THE IMPORTANCE OF DECISION-MAKING

Dramatic tension is held if the story develops through decisions made by the main characters. It is not held if the story develops through coincidence and arbitrary accidents. When that happens it ceases to be a story and becomes a succession of incidents.

The viewers need to see a central character faced with a problem. They need to see the options available. They need to see a decision taken – and then to see the result. If a character has to achieve a goal you should put as many obstacles as possible in his path, force him to take as many decisions as possible, and then show how he copes.

Arbitrary accidents can form obstacles – the cork-extractor man from New Jersey might be speeding across Africa in a train that breaks down. But this is a device to offer a new decision to be taken: does he wait for the train to be mended or hitch a ride on a poorly looking camel owned by a one-eyed bandit with a sharp knife? If he goes on the camel, will it collapse, or will the bandit kill him?

It is important that decisions should be left to your central characters. In this case the bandit must either be innocent of evil intent, or waiting to pounce. It will almost certainly not work if you switch the focus, and have the bandit making a decision: do I kill this cork-extractor man or not? If I do will I escape with his money or get caught?

It will also be profoundly unsatisfactory if the man from New Jersey fails to reach the man with the corked arse because he catches a cold and has to go to bed, where a snake that we knew nothing about bites him and he dies.

CONSEQUENCES OF ACTION: CAUSE AND EFFECT

> The King died and then the Queen died. That is a story. The King died and then the Queen died of *grief*. That is a plot.
>
> (E. M. Forster, *Aspects of the Novel*)

People who write about, and lecture on, creative writing, often go on at great length about the difference between plot and story. It really doesn't matter. It's not going to make the slightest different to your script. But at its simplest, the plot is what makes your story happen. It is cause and effect: you set up a situation and then see how your characters react to it, and thus a new situation, and event, is created.

CREATING SYMPATHY

It is useful to have at least *one* sympathetic character and to introduce him at an early stage. Viewers like to know who to identify with, they like to know who they should be cheering for. You can, of course, show a pleasant character and later reveal a vicious side to his nature – and you can have a vile person who turns out to have all kinds of redeeming features. But at the beginning of a play we need to establish something, or somebody, that viewers can *care about*.

> The 'story' is what actually happens, the material of the tale, and the 'plot' is the way a narrative is realised.
>
> (Patricia Holland, *The Television Handbook*)

PLOTS TO AVOID

The idiot plot

Script editors hate plots which can only work if basically intelligent characters behave in a totally stupid way. *Dr Who* was (and indeed still is) a terrible culprit here – the Doctor and his Assistant would be clinging to each other in some noisome underground cave system, we would *all know* they ought to stay together, but sure enough the Doctor would say: 'I'll be back in a minute', and wander off on his own, leaving his assistant to be captured and held prisoner for the next four episodes. In *Dr Who* this was expected, it was part of the formula, but it is basically very lazy plotting.

Story development should stem from character. You should never force characters unnaturally to obey your plot.

Scenes that go nowhere

Every scene should move the story on. It should advance the plot or illuminate the characters – preferably both. Beware of scenes that repeat the plot but in a slightly different way. If you write a scene, and then find you can cut it out of your script without losing anything relevant to the story, then cut it.

Plots that lose tension

We must always want to know what is going to happen next. If a scene satisfies curiosity roused in previous scenes, it should also arouse curiosity about events in the future. Plots often lose tension because:

◆ you have resolved conflict elements too soon, and there is nothing left for us to anticipate

◆ your plot has become bogged down in explanations of past events; viewers are rarely kept on the edge of their seats by verbal explanations of what has gone before

◆ it was a boring idea to start with.

SUMMARY

◆ The 'plot' is the order of events in which you choose to tell the 'story'.

◆ All drama depends on conflict – but conflict does not have to mean aggression.

◆ Do not devise plots that can only work if your characters are stupid. Never force characters unnaturally to obey your plot.

◆ Do not let your plot get bogged down in verbal explanations of previous scenes.

6

Visual Interest

You have come up with a brilliant idea, and you have worked out a plot showing how the story will develop. The third thing you need to be able to do is to *tell your story in an interesting way.*

This chapter will look at:

- ◆ visual interest on screen
- ◆ using pictures instead of words
- ◆ ways to maintain dramatic tension
- ◆ opening scenes of a *Boon* episode.

HOW TO INCREASE VISUAL INTEREST

Watch any popular drama series on ITV and note how short most scenes are, how quickly we move about, and how few scenes take place in visually boring places like offices or sitting rooms (in other words locations reminiscent of studio plays). In *Peacemaker*, the *Boon* episode looked at in this chapter, there are only three scenes set in the detective agency's office. When a director comes across a wordy, static indoor scene with two people talking to each other, his first instinct is to move the scene to somewhere else: somewhere visually interesting. The longer and more wordy (or delicate and sensitive as you the writer might put it) the scene, the more he will want to break it up with movement, and before you know it your characters will be playing squash or practising on the high trapeze. Even if restrained from his wilder notions, the director would rather have characters walking sedately along a river bank than sitting on opposite sides of a table. This gives him *variety of shots* and allows him to punctuate the dramatic content of the scene with *movement*.

You give the director this:

INT. KITCHEN. DAY.   MARY AND JOHN ARE STILL SITTING AT THE KITCHEN TABLE. HIS HEAD IS SLUMPED.

MARY: John? If you've got something to say then I'd rather you said it.

JOHN LOOKS UP

JOHN: OK. All right. I've been having an affair with Tracy from the catfood factory.

MARY TURNS AWAY SHARPLY. JOHN PAUSES, SHATTERED FOR A MOMENT HAVING FINALLY BROUGHT HIMSELF TO TELL HER. THEN HE CONTINUES WITH NEW CONFI-DENCE:

We love each other and I want a divorce. I want children and you can't give me children. I know it's not your fault, I know that you desperately want children yourself, but there's no reason for us both to suffer –

MARY: Stop it, stop it, stop it!

And the director gives you back this:

EXT. RIVERBANK. DAY

MARY AND JOHN WALK ON PAST THE WEIR, UNDER THE FALLING LEAVES OF AUTUMN. THEY ARE STILL SILENT WITH MISERY. MARY STOPS AND THROWS BREAD TO A SWAN AND HER CYGNETS.

MARY: John? (HE DOES NOT RESPOND) If you've got something to say then I'd rather you said it.

JOHN: OK. All right. I've been having an affair with Tracy from the catfood factory.

MARY FREEZES. THE MOTHER SWAN AND HER CYGNETS ARE EATING THE BREAD. JOHN PAUSES SHATTERED FOR A MOMENT HAVING FINALLY BROUGHT HIMSELF TO TELL HER. THEN HE CONTINUES WITH NEW CONFIDENCE. WE WATCH THE SWAN AND HER CYGNETS FROM MARY'S POV:

JOHN: (OOV)   We love each other
and I want a divorce. I want children, and you can't
give me children. I know it's not your fault, I know
that you desperately want children yourself, but there's
no reason for us both to suffer –

CUT SHARPLY BACK TO MARY WHO TURNS

MARY: Stop it, stop it, stop it!

THE SWAN FLAPS HER WINGS IN ALARM
AND HER CYGNETS SCATTER.

The second version allows the story to progress visually
(in this scene we are at the weir, in a previous scene we
would have been on another part of the river bank);
allows us to have a decent dramatic pause for John and
still have something to look at; gives us a nice bit of
symbolism looking at a Mum and her little ones while
John cruelly rambles on about childlessness; and the
ominous rumble of the weir in the background offers a
hint that Mary might either drown herself or, preferably,
drown John.

USING PICTURES INSTEAD OF WORDS
Before writing a word of dialogue, always ask yourself
whether any dialogue is necessary at all.

(Malcolm Hulke, writer)

Picture the following scene:

A group round a coffin in a country graveyard. The

vicar intoning from the *Book of Common Prayer*. We see the Range Rovers and the BMWs parked on the verges of the country lane, the rooks cawing round their nests in the dead elm trees. The camera PANS along thoughtful, sober faces, until it finds JASPER, who is surreptitiously smiling behind his asthma inhaler.

Cut to DOLORES, who shoots him a glance of pure hate.

CUT TO: Shovels of earth fall on the coffin. The rooks caw, the vicar intones, and we suddenly become aware of heavy laboured breathing... the breathing of somebody struggling for life.

CUT TO: The rooks wheel round the elms.

CUT TO: JASPER begins to turn blue, his breath wheezing. Somebody screams. JASPER falls into the open grave.

CUT TO: DOLORES turns away. Her hand lightly checks the side pocket of her Burberry, to make sure the zip is fastened. She strolls towards the church gate.

We don't need a competition to see how pictures here can substitute for words in setting the scene (England, C of E, middle-class, rural, springtime because the rooks are nesting, a burial) and also in telling the story (Jasper murdered by Dolores who has the asthma inhaler poison in her Burberry pocket) – and all without a word of dialogue apart from the words of Archbishop Cranmer, who is out of copyright anyway.

Looking at the scenes from *Peacemaker on* pages 61–71 you will see how the scenes with dialogue are punctuated by scenes which move the story along purely with the use of pictures.

DRAMATIC TENSION

You must always have something on screen that holds the interest of the viewer. It might be one of the following:

◆ **A development of the plot** – our attention is held because we have become involved in the characters and the story, and we want to know what will happen next.

◆ **Emotion** – happiness, shock, tears. It is distressing but true that people are fascinated by other people's emotional reactions.

◆ **Humour** – an interlude involving a humorous theme might not move the plot forward or reveal anything new, but providing we laugh all can be forgiven. In *Peacemaker* we have two pop concert promoters who have 'lost' their star – and Boon is trying to find him. We need to cut back to the promoters now and again, simply so that we will not forget their existence. In plot terms the obvious thing would be to show them sitting in their sordid office, waiting – or on the phone to our detectives demanding to know what was happening. Instead the writers run a small sub-theme in which the promoters' sidekick tries to prove his cleverness by suggesting alternative stars. In one scene he is inspired to utter the words 'Gary Glitter', and the promoter opens the window and howls like a soul in torture; in another he modestly suggests his younger brother, and the promoter snarls: 'I've billed this as a comeback. How can your brother come back? He hasn't been anywhere.'

◆ **Visual interest** – by providing movement, rapid cuts from location to location, interesting locations, people running, vehicles moving at speed. What we see on the screen can help sustain dramatic tension.

Things that lose dramatic tension

◆ Scenes or fragments of dialogue that do not go anywhere, and do not relate to the story or plot.

◆ Scenes that repeat themselves and fail to move the story on.

◆ Characters that fail to react in a logical manner. To a considerable extent viewers look to the reactions of characters in a play in order to work out their own reactions. If a woman hits a man in a restaurant and nobody pays any attention, and the man carries on eating his food, then there will be no dramatic tension. But if the entire restaurant falls silent, and the man stares in cold fury and the woman begins to shake – then there is dramatic tension.

A LOOK AT THE OPENING OF A *BOON* EPISODE

We've looked at some elements that go into telling a story on television. Now take a look at a professional script.

Boon was a Central Television drama series about a private detective, Ken Boon, played by Michael Elphick. It was comedy-drama, but occasionally with a hard edge. Six series were made and the programme moved locations during each series. An outstanding episode was *Peacemaker* written by Diane Culverhouse and Julian Spilsbury for Series Three.

At the time Ken Boon and Margaret Daley were partners in a small Birmingham private detective agency. The agency's office was at the back of the Plaza Suite – a run-down function venue owned by Ken's old friend Harry.

The main story in *Peacemaker* opens with the following situation: A Midland pop star, Bograt, is due to attend a 'comeback' recording session in Birmingham. He loses his nerve and disappears. The promoters hire Boon and Margaret to track him down.

How would you write the first scene, explaining the situation?

The following openings were suggested by students at a television drama seminar.

Suggestion one:
Boon's office. CLOSE UP of a newspaper with a photograph of Bograt and headline 'Comeback for Brum pop star'. PULL BACK to show promoter asking Boon and Margaret to take on the case.

The use of the newspaper picture is good, but otherwise this is a very boring, non-visual opening that does little to whet our curiosity and depends on our absorbing a lot of information through dialogue rather than pictures.

Suggestion two:
Bograt arrives at Birmingham railway station, or airport, and is surrounded by fans. As he leaves the station he is pounced on and pushed into a car that disappears at speed.

Nice and visual and it ought to arouse our curiosity – but Bograt is supposed to disappear in panic, not be kidnapped. All right, he could have set up the kidnap himself, but why come back to Birmingham at all in that case? Is he, perhaps, going into hiding just to seek publicity?

Trying to find a logical motivation for the visually-interesting kidnap is changing the entire storyline – and we are only in scene one!

This opening adds a further complication: the disappearance is now public knowledge, and one area of dramatic tension – only a small group of people aware that he has disappeared has been lost to us.

Suggestion three:
Bograt on stage at a comeback concert. It's a huge success/miserable failure. Backstage afterwards the promoter goes to Bograt's dressing room and finds it empty ... and the window open.

This is good and visual. The concert must, presumably, be a success or the promoter is not going to care whether Bograt disappears or not. But if it is a success, then Bograt has already made his comeback – and to some extent at least the story is over. Also, if it is a success, why has he done a bunk?

On a practical level, it is hugely expensive to hire a theatre, put in lighting, stage a pop concert, and fill the theatre with people just to get 30 seconds of material.

Here is how the writers of Peacemaker tackled the opening, and also how they introduced the other stories in the episode.

1. EXT. BIRMINGHAM STREET. NIGHT.
A LARGE HOTEL, THERE IS LOUD, HEAVY METAL MUSIC FROM AN UPPER FLOOR WINDOW. THE MUSIC STOPS ABRUPTLY. THERE IS SHOUTING. A WINDOW BREAKS. A BLACK LEATHERY FIGURE (BOGRAT) EMERGES AND RACES DOWN A FIRE ESCAPE.

WE SEE HIS FACE BRIEFLY BEFORE HE LOPES OFF INTO THE NIGHT.

2. INT. MARGARET'S BEDROOM. NIGHT.
MARGARET IN BED ASLEEP IS WOKEN BY THE PHONE RINGING. SHE PICKS UP THE RECEIVER, GRUMPILY LOOKING AT THE CLOCK.

MARGARET: Hello?... Speaking... (WINCES) What, now? Yes, I know it.... I'll be right round. (SLIGHTLY INCREDULOUS) What did you say his name was?

3. INT. HOTEL LUXURY SUITE. NIGHT.
PROMOTIONAL MATERIAL ADVERTISES THE 'BOGRAT AND THE NEKROS' COMEBACK ALBUM. BOGRAT FEATURES PROMINENTLY. THE ROOM IS A SCENE OF DEVASTATION. THE MINI FRIDGE IS DRY, THE DOOR HANGS OFF. BOTTLES, CANS, CIGARETTE ENDS LITTER EVERY SURFACE. BOGRAT'S MANAGER LENNY BRIGHT IS STUMPING ANGRILY ROUND THE ROOM. GEOFF, HIS GOPHER, IS JUST FINISHING THE CALL TO MARGARET. A GIRL, NIKKI, IS SPACED OUT AND SOBBING. THE MEN IGNORE HER.

GEOFF: She's coming straight over.

LENNY: Nice work, Geoff.

GEOFF: I only turned my back for five minutes!

LENNY: He didn't need five minutes. (Thinks) Were you with a bird?

GEOFF: (FOLLOWING HIM AROUND THE ROOM) it was a call of nature. The en suite was full.

LENNY: (PEERS INTO BATH-
ROOM) Good grief. (TURNS AWAY) It still is.

THE HOTEL MANAGER ENTERS AND LOOKS
ROUND IN HORROR AT THE DEVASTATION.

MANAGER: Oh my god!

LENNY: (TO GEOFF) Pay the
man.

GEOFF GOES OVER DRAGGING OUT HIS
WALLET

4. EXT. BIRMINGHAM STREET. NIGHT
A POLICE CAR, SIREN GOING, PULLS UP AT A
PUNCH-UP OUTSIDE A SEEDY NIGHT CLUB.
THE BLACK LEATHERY FIGURE OF BOGRAT
SURVEYS THE SCENE WITH EVIDENT SATIS-
FACTION, THEN TURNS AND WALKS AWAY.

HE LOOKS ROUND HIM AT THE TATTY
STREETS, THEN PUNCHES THE AIR AND
JUMPS FOR JOY. HE IS HOME, AND HE IS FREE.

5. INT. HOTEL LOBBY. NIGHT
MARGARET CROSSES FOYER AND ENTERS
LIFT.

6. INT. HOTEL SUITE. OUTER ROOM. NIGHT
GEOFF IS BUYING OFF THE HOTEL MAN-
AGER. THERE IS A PILE OF £20 NOTES

BETWEEN THEM TO WHICH GEOFF KEEPS
ADDING. BEHIND THEM SITS NIKKI, STILL
SOBBING AND IGNORED.

MANAGER: Carpets. Duvets...

MARGARET ENTERS

MARGARET: Mr Bright?

GEOFF: Just follow the wreckage. (TO MANAGER) Where were we?

MARGARET GOES THROUGH TO THE INNER
ROOM.

MANAGER: Carpets.

GEOFF: Two-hundred-and-fifty.

NIKKI: I'm going to be sick!

MANAGER: No you don't!

HE DIVES TOWARDS HER. GEOFF SLIPS A
COUPLE OF NOTES BACK OFF THE PILE.

7. INT. HOTEL LUXURY SUITE. INNER ROOM.
NIGHT

LENNY: Lenny Bright. 'Bright
Ideas'.

MARGARET: I understand you're
missing a lead singer.

LENNY: (GESTURES TO A
POSTER) You remember the Nekros?

MARGARET: (TACTFUL) Perhaps
you'd refresh my memory.

LENNY: Split up five years ago,
I've got them back together. Or at least, I had got them
back together.

MARGARET: Well done.

LENNY: We're doing a come-back album, but it
won't be worth a fart in a thunderstorm without *him*.

MARGARET: Bograt?

LENNY: You see? You do remember! That's what
makes him special. I found him in Calais.

MARGARET: Calais?

LENNY: (NODS) It'll be
engraved on my heart too.

MARGARET: What was he doing in
Calais?

LENNY: On his way to Monte

Carlo. He'd been on his way to Monte Carlo for five years. It was as far as he got.

MARGARET: And now he's gone again?

LENNY: Has a bust up with his girlfriend and (POINTS TO WINDOW) vroom!

MARGARET: Couldn't he use a door like anyone else?

LENNY: He isn't like anyone else!

MARGARET: And you want me to find him?

LENNY: And fast! I've got a studio, session artists, a producer, all standing idle.

MARGARET: (LOOKS AT POSTER) Is this fairly recent?

LENNY: We've a video in the office that's better.

MARGARET: I'll send somebody round for it. (LOOKS AT NIKKI, WHO IS NOW BEING TENDED BY GEOFF) I take it that's the girlfriend?

LENNY: (NODS) How is she, Geoff?

GEOFF: (WAVES A HAND IN FRONT OF HER FACE) Nikki? (NO RESPONSE) The lights are on but there's no one in.

MARGARET: I'll talk to her in the morning. Mr Bright, this won't be easy. If somebody really wants to hide –

LENNY: I want you on this full time. Usual rates. Two hundred quid bonus if you get him within forty-eight hours.

MARGARET: But he could be out of the country by morning.

LENNY SHAKES HIS HEAD. HE DRAWS HER TO THE WINDOW. HE TURNS OFF THE LIGHT. THEY LOOK OUT OVER BIRMINGHAM AT NIGHT, AND WE LOOK WITH THEM. LENNY'S VOICE CHOKES WITH EMOTION.

LENNY: That's what brought him back. That city crouched down there like a beast. Those streets, those subways, they gave him everything. Life, art, inspiration. This is his city. Bograt's town.

8. INT. PLAZA SUITE. DAY
HARRY IS IN HIS BEST SUIT. HIS MINIONS

ARE PREPARING A PROMOTION FOR A DUTCH MACHINE TOOL COMPANY. THERE ARE LITTLE DUTCH FLAGS, BUNCHES OF PLASTIC TULIPS, AND A DUTCH-STYLE BUFFET BEING LAID OUT BY LINDA. HARRY CROSSES TO HER, HOLDING A LITTLE DUTCH PHRASE BOOK.

HARRY: Linda, what do you think 'Ik geloof dat ik voed-selvergiftiging hab' means?

LINDA: How about 'Go away and let me finish this buffet in peace?'

HARRY: (LAUGHS) Very close! Actually it's 'I think I've got food poisoning.'

HARRY SAMPLES SOMETHING FROM A PLATE. LINDA SNATCHES IT AWAY.

LINDA: Actually that pumpernickel's in short supply, Mr Crawford.

HARRY: (PULLS FACE) I'm glad to hear it. (CALLS) Can you put the music on now?

MARGARET HAS WALKED IN. HARRY APPROACHES HER. SHE LOOKS TIRED.

HARRY: Morning Margaret. Or should I say 'Goede Morgen'?

MARGARET: Very good. Who's coming, Queen Beatrix?

HARRY: A big machine-tool company from Utrecht, here for the week. Quite a coup, actually.

MARGARET: You've certainly done them proud. All you need now is

THE MUSIC STARTS UP. IT IS MAX BYGRAVES SINGING 'TULIPS FROM AMSTERDAM'.

MARGARET: (FINISHES SEN-TENCE) Max Bygraves singing 'Tulips from Amsterdam'.

HARRY WINKS AT HER. HE IS ONE UP.

9. INT. BDI OFFICE. PLAZA SUITE. DAY
KEN IS TALKING TO A NERVOUS YOUNG WOMAN, WE CAN STILL HEAR THE MUSIC AND SO CAN THEY. THE WOMAN TURNS TO LOOK IN THE DIRECTION OF THE NOISE.

ELAINE: (SMILES SADLY) We went there on our honeymoon.

KEN: (SMILES COM-FORTINGLY, REFERS TO HIS NOTES). This business 'Luxor Bathroom Fittings'. Does he own it?

ELAINE: No. He's the branch manager.

KEN: Still, he's doing all right?

ELAINE: Doing very well by all accounts. (SIGHS) I sound like a money-grabbing bitch, don't I?

KEN: Course not. The court awarded you maintenance.

MARGARET ENTERS

MARGARET: Morning Ken, we've got the most amazing... oh, I beg your pardon.

KEN: Mrs Bache, this is my partner, Margaret Daley.

ELAINE: How do you do.

MARGARET: Hello. I'll leave you to it.

SHE COLLECTS UP HER POST, SMILES AND EXITS.

ELAINE: (ON VERGE OF TEARS) I've got bills to pay. And if he's earning more than he says he's earning, well it's not fair, is it?

KEN: You're sure that's
what he's doing?

ELAINE: Well I can't afford to
go gadding round town all the time.

KEN: And he can?

ELAINE: That's what I've heard.

KEN: Women?

ELAINE: I don't know. Friends
don't like to tell you about other women, do they?

KEN: No, still, it's possible.
(LOOKS AT PHOTOGRAPH) He's not a bad-looking
bloke, is he?

ELAINE: Appearances can be
very deceptive. He's a bastard, Mr Boon. A real
bastard.

How does the opening of Peacemaker work?

Scene One
The opening is visual and fast moving, from the window
smashing to the darkened figure racing down the fire
escape. The fire escape sequence also allows time for the
opening titles.

Scene Two
In one line we establish that the Boon agency is being

involved and that the matter is urgent. Curiosity is roused by the incredulous: 'What did you say his name was?'

Scene Three
In only eight lines of dialogue we are given two points of conflict and a second story strand is established:

- Lenny blames Geoff for losing Bograt, Geoff is resentful
- the hotel manager is horrified by the wreckage: Geoff is told to sort him out.

Scene Four
Bograt, enjoying his freedom. It is totally visual but tells us a lot about his character and the situation he is in.

Scene Five
Again is totally visual, showing Margaret arriving at the hotel.

Scene Six and Scene Seven
The basic situation is explained to Margaret – but note how we have the secondary story of Geoff and the hotel manager to divert us – the manager demanding heavy payment, Geoff doling the money out, Nikki the girlfriend almost being sick, Geoff pinching back some money, Nikki collapsing in a drunken stupor.

Note how future development is set up: Margaret asks if a poster is recent, Lenny says he has a video, Margaret says she'll send somebody round for it.

Scene Eight

A very visual scene with Dutch flags, tulips and buffet in the Plaza Suite sets up the comic subplot and brings Margaret in.

Scene Nine

The mood changes entirely as the second main story is set up. The music 'Tulips from Amsterdam' links the two scenes – but now has sad connotations. This scene has to give solid information, but note how it is given to us through natural dialogue – through the nervousness and distress of Elaine and how the scene ends with an ominous warning for the future: 'He's a bastard, Mr Boon, a real bastard'. Also note that although the scene is only two pages long, it has been broken up by the entry of Margaret.

All three stories have now been introduced – and we have learned as much through the eye of the camera as through dialogue.

SUMMARY

- Avoid long scenes full of verbal explanation.

- Avoid long indoor scenes set in one room.

- Whenever possible use pictures rather than words to tell your story.

- Moving quickly between short scenes will increase pace and maintain tension.

7

Dialogue

THE THREE FUNCTIONS OF DIALOGUE

Dialogue is traditionally said to have three functions.

1. **To advance the story**. Just as each scene in a play should move the story forward, so each line of dialogue – or sequence of lines should also move the plot onwards. Dialogue which repeats itself, or tells us things we know already, or gets bogged down in side issues, will destroy the dramatic tension of the scene.

2. **To reveal character**. A good line not only moves the story forward, it also reveals some facet, however minor, of the speaker's personality. See how Anna's character emerges from the two speeches quoted on page 76.

3. **To give us information**. Good dialogue gives us a mass of information – but without us realising it. If you look at the opening of the *Boon* episode on page 61 you will see how few words have actually been used to set up three stories and introduce half a dozen characters.

HOW TO CREATE CHARACTER THROUGH DIALOGUE

Everyone speaks differently, uses different vocabulary,

different speech patterns. The characters in your play should be identifiable by their speech and the expressions they use. A common piece of advice is: after you have written a page of dialogue put a ruler over the names of the characters and then see if you can identify the speakers from their words alone.

Intelligence, class, education, geographical background – all these things contribute to the way people speak. It is a useful dramatic device to give characters expressions of their own: the most famous perhaps being Walter Gabriel's 'Me old pal me old beauty' in *The Archers*, or references to 'She who must be obeyed' in *Rumpole*. Read *The Importance of Being Earnest* and see that for all Wilde's stylisation, the languid speech patterns of Lady Bracknell contrast with the down-to-earth speech of Gwendoline.

COLOUR AND TEXTURE

The barge she sat in, like a burnish'd throne,
Burn'd on the water; the poop was beaten gold,
Purple the sails, and so perfumed, that
The winds were love-sick with them, the oars were silver
Which to the tune of flutes kept stroke, and made
The water which they beat to follow faster,
As amorous of their strokes.

(Shakespeare, *Anthony and Cleopatra*)

Most television dialogue imitates documentary realism, and you are not expected to be overly lyrical in your average *Casualty* or *Eastenders*. But dialogue needs colour and texture. However naturalistic on the surface, it needs to paint pictures with words. In the script layout example on page 191 a girl desperately in love with a nuclear disarmament supporter tells us that she has been on a protest march. In terms of plot all she needs to say is: 'I went on a march'. But the writer tells us much more than that:

> ANNA... I went on a march – my red slingbacks with four-inch heels all though London, past all the shops and I didn't go in, not even down Sloane Street.

In a single line we are given a picture of Anna on her march, tottering along in red slingbacks with her eyes on the shop windows rather than the protest banners. In an earlier scene in the play Anna admits that she is not actually interested in nuclear disarmament. Her friend Daisy says: 'I'm not convinced your heart's in it' and the simple, flat answer would be: 'No, you're right, it isn't.' In the script, though, we get:

> ANNA: of course it isn't – the whole thing's totally tedious. I'm not interested in aeroplanes and fighting and wars – that's boys' stuff. American bases and NATO bases and all the bombs have got daft names and numbers. Why hasn't Simon noticed me?

Quality of dialogue, expressed through vocabulary and images, is what stamps your own signature on a script. If you gave Lucy Gannon, Andrew Davies, and Alan Bennett an identical subject on which to write, they would all produce excellent, well-structured, well-characterised plays – but each would be totally different. This would be caused largely by their different views of life, but we would be made most aware of it through each writer's distinctive dialogue.

ECONOMY WITH WORDS

When Oscar Wilde said he had spent all morning deciding to put a comma in a sentence, and all afternoon deciding to take it out, he was probably telling no more than the truth.

In a film or television script every word should count. Every word should have its purpose. Once you have written a scene, go back through it and see how many lines you can lose, how many words you can strike out without losing either plot, atmosphere, or characterization. You must be your own first script editor – and the more ruthless you are the better.

Dramatic dialogue is superficially naturalistic, but in fact is highly artificial. In real life people 'um' and they 'ah', they don't finish their sentences, they employ a surprisingly limited vocabulary, and they generally use ten words where one will do.

The art of television dialogue is to write something that sounds naturalistic, but in which every word has a place and a purpose.

> Most people said how vivid and realistic the Liverpool dialogue was in *No Trains to Lime Street*. In fact, no one in Liverpool ever spoke as I make them speak in the play.
>
> (Alun Owen)

SUBTEXT

Subtext sounds a bit technical and advanced – it's the sort of word (the favourite is **genre**) that script editors like to use. Really it is very simple. The subtext is the meaning that is being conveyed, when the meaning is different from the words actually spoken.

When the lecher sidles up to the girl on a dusky summer's evening and murmurs: 'Why don't we go into the garden and look at the Old English roses?' and she looks him coolly up and down before smiling discreetly and saying: 'Yes, why not?' – we know full well that they are not anticipating a chat about horticulture and ways to combat greenfly.

And when another girl hears the conversation and watches them leave and turns indignantly to another person and says: 'My God, did you see that? What an oily bastard – and what a tart she is!', we know that elements of personal jealousy are bubbling beneath the surface.

The commonly quoted example of subtext through pictures is the scene in the film *Tom Jones* where Tom and Mrs Waters eat a meal with their fingers in an outrageously seductive manner. The pictures show them devouring their food; the subtext tells us that they are devouring each other.

THE THROUGH LINE

The first thing an actor does when he opens a script is to see how big his part is. The next thing he looks for is a 'through line' for his character.

He is looking for a logical progress of thoughts and ideas. He can only memorise his lines if one thought leads to another thought, one exchange of dialogue leads, logically, to another. Actors find lines difficult to learn if the thoughts and expressions are illogical or repetitive.

'BAD LANGUAGE'

Language is extraordinarily powerful; much more powerful than pictures. A BBC survey in 1987 showed that strong disapproval of bad language exceeded strong disapproval of sex on television by a margin of three to one. Television transmits into people's homes, where three generations, from children to grandparents, might be watching at the same time. Television companies therefore have to be careful about the language they use.

There is an evening watershed at nine o'clock. Before then certain words cannot – or should not – be used. Both the BBC and IBA have from time to time graded words according to their offensiveness. In a recent ruling 'bollocks' was not approved before nine o'clock but, curiously, 'bugger' and 'piss off' were all right in small doses. 'Shag' was only allowable before nine if it referred to tobacco or the common cormorant. 'Fuck' could not be said at all.

Times change. Some children's dramas – meaningful, socially relevant ones – now sometimes include phrases like 'piss off' and words like 'arsehole', while 'fuck off' is heard on terrestrial television after nine o'clock. Satellite television now shows feature films that have not been expurgated.

The new writer needs a good story and good dialogue but providing it is justified, the use of gutsy language wi not do any harm. A few 'bollocks' will meet with mos script editors' approval; it gives them something t champion, and lets them think they are advancing th cause of television drama. And at the end of the day the can always cut them out.

COMMON FAULTS IN DIALOGUE

Unsayable lines

New writers often write dialogue that looks fine on pape but is actually very difficult to say. Read your lines ou loud to see how well they work. Avoid not only tongu twisters like 'the Leith Police dismisseth us', bu convoluted lines, repetitiv lines, and lines with a grea number of very short word 'I'll just ask if they don't min us going out to find out wha was going on.' (Mind you, you do write a line as bad a that you might as well give up

> Writing film and TV plays – that is writing dramatic dialogue – absolutely demands that the writer should be alive to the sound of everyday speech.
> (Rodney Bennett, director)

This is not to say you can't repeat words and phrases:

> DICK: OK, all right, that's it then Sunbeam, you'v done it this time, this time you are in real trouble, o yes you are in real trouble...

says our angry policeman moving rapidly across the ce and grabbing his victim by the throat.

Dialogue should be alive, it should sparkle. It has been described as the 'nerve ends of feelings', it is usually based on emotional responses, and if it is well written it gives pace and energy to the script.

Use of dialect
It is risky to get enmeshed in dialect and foreign accents. A play written in dialect is pretty well guaranteed to make a script editor's eyes glaze over. Italians crying 'Mama Mia' and Frenchmen shouting 'Allez mes enfants!' are nearly as off-putting as Yorkshiremen saying 'Ahm gerrin off down't pit but a'l sithi' in't mornin'. Regional cliches ('By gum, it's a bit parky tonight, mother') are also best avoided, and the example of dialogue below not only shows us the awfulness of fake dialect but also demonstrates another fault common in many scripts:

GEORGE: Shall us have our tea now then Martha?

MARTHA: Aye if tha's ready George.

GEORGE: Wilt have an egg wi' bacon for tha's tea Martha?

MARTHA: If that's what tha's having George.

GEORGE: Ah thinks ah'll have a sausage, Martha.

MARTHA: You have what tha' bloody well likes, George.

The additional fault is:

Overuse of character names
A common fault is for characters to call each other by

name to an extent that is not credible. In real life w
rarely need to tag a person's name on to the end of
sentence, and in conversation most people only use
person's name to create intimacy or to emphasise th
importance of what they are saying. A woman might say
'John, that is not true. I swear to you that I was nowher
near Randy Ron's house last night', or a man might say
'I'm sorry Michele, I really am.'

Pseudo dialect, badly chosen character names (see pag
91) and overuse of character names can ruin dialogue tha
might otherwise be perfectly acceptable. Look at th
dialogue between George and Martha if the dialect i
taken out, the characters given different names and th
passage put in a dramatic framework.

> GILLIAN's nerves are at breaking point. Her father
> in-law TOM has been staying in the house since th
> death of her husband PATRICK in an accident thre
> weeks ago. TOM is a widower in his late eighties
> bewildered and lost – GILLIAN tries to be kind, bu
> all she wants is to be alone.
>
> GILLIAN sits staring into the empty fireplace. TOM
> looks at her once or twice.
>
> TOM: Shall we have som
> tea?
>
> GILLIAN: If you're ready.
>
> She does not move. TOM says nothing for a momen
> then tries to speak brightly.

TOM: Will you have some
eggs and bacon?

GILLIAN: If that's what you're
having.

She still does not look up.

TOM: I think I'll have a
sausage.

GILLIAN: Have what you bloody
well like!

Silence. Slowly, GILLIAN starts to cry.

SUMMARY

Every line of dialogue should advance the story, reveal the character of the person speaking, or give us background information. A good line will do all three things.

Every word you write should be necessary or should be cut.

Dialogue should sound totally natural unless you are writing in a deliberately stylised manner (not recommended: script editors will simply think that you can't write).

The more you can make your dialogue fresh, lively and vivid the better.

Avoid dialect.

Avoid over-using character names.

Say lines out loud, or in your head, as you write them.

$$8$$

Characterisation

GIVING CHARACTERS DEPTH

A common note of dismissal on rejected scripts is: 'characters two dimensional' or 'cardboard characters'. This means that the characters do not 'come off the page' as rounded, interesting, individual personalities. It is not always easy to give characters depth when everything they do, or say, must somehow advance the story. Here are some hints:

- Avoid stereotypes. For example, do not have retired colonels who cry 'What? What?' in peppery voices and complain about young people today.

- Give even minor characters more than one aspect to their nature. This does not have to be extreme – you do not have to give a vicar a penchant for roulette and girls – but remember that people are made up of a complex mixture of likes, dislikes, strengths, weaknesses and moral views.

- At its simplest, if you have a postman who appears two or three times in your script, and whose only function is to deliver letters critical to your plot, decide: is he a happy postman? Or a miserable postman? Does he perhaps whistle, and if so, what sort of tune? A whistling postman is a bit of a cliche, but what if he's a dour, miserable-looking postman who always whistles 'The Sun has got his hat on, hip-hip-hip-hurray?' You will, *without a single line of dialogue*, have given your postman an intriguing feature, a personality.

◆ A cunning if weary old ploy used by professional writers is to give the hero a minor failing (a detective hero who can't resist cream buns) and the villain a minor virtue (a gangster with a secret passion for Gilbert and Sullivan operettas). This technique can give the script the appearance, at least, of depth of characterisation.

◆ You can sometimes rescue a cliched character late on in a script by adding unexpected humour and self-awareness. Your peppery colonel mutters 'Dear God, young people today! His wife says, 'Why do you *always* have to say that?' He replies musingly, 'I've no idea. Perhaps because it's expected of me', and his wife stares at him in amazement. This technique gives you the advantage of the stereotype (viewers know exactly where they are) with the added virtue of dramatic revelation as a new side to the colonel's character is revealed.

DEVELOPING CHARACTERS

The development of character is an important part of any drama, indeed most dramas are not about action but about reaction, not about car chases and murder but about the effect such events have on the attitudes of the people who survive them.

> Every single character, even a bastard like Goldberg in *The Birthday Party*, I care for.
>
> (Harold Pinter)

The important thing is to build the different facets of a person's personality into a coherent whole. The actor studying the part will be looking for a **through line** of character development (see page 78). If the character in question is mild and sensible at the beginning of the play, but ends up smashing the furniture and butchering the cat, then the actor will:

- want to know why his character has changed

- want to understand the thought processes that have led to the change

- look for the key line, possibly by another character ('People forget George's unpredictable temper, but it's always there, it's not gone away') that will help to understand why he has turned into a cat-murdering fiend

- go back to the beginning – and create a performance from the start which allows the character later to reveal hidden emotional depths.

Actors become frustrated when they find in one scene that they are good-natured, and in another scene that they are not – but cannot find any explanation in the script.

ILL-TREATING CHARACTERS

Writers can do terrible things to their characters. They create creatures that live and breathe – and then destroy them, carelessly or ruthlessly, to maintain their plot, or to save a scene that is looking sticky, or because they can't think what to do next and making a character do something highly peculiar will cause a temporary sensation.

There are two forms of character sacrifice to beware of:

♦ sacrificing character for plot
♦ sacrificing character for sensation.

Sacrificing your characters for plot

The most common fault is to make formerly intelligent characters behave stupidly for no reason (see the idiot plot, page 50), or to make characters behave out of character because the plot demands it.

Perhaps your story is that of a 16-year-old girl who is pregnant and who is frightened to tell anyone. You want us to see her attempting to confide in a succession of people, including her mother.

ELVA: The thing is Mum –

MUM: Just look at your father! I don't know what he thinks he's doing!

ELVA: I'm in trouble..real trouble –

MUM: Out there in this wind without his pullover on!

ELVA: I've got to tell you; I'll go mad if I don't tell somebody.

MUM: Just go and give him a shout, Elva – I know I like fresh brussels sprouts but if he gets one of his colds we'll hear about it for weeks.

Mum here is presumably stone deaf and stupid – all very well, but elsewhere in the play we may have found her to be a perfectly normal, reasonably intelligent person. The writer *needs* Elva to fail to communicate so that she can be rejected by the world (and so that the play will run for a full 50 minutes), so in this particular scene Mum's character as a sane human being is sacrificed to make the plot work. A similar occurrence is likely to happen in the doctor's surgery:

ELVA: (Whispers) I'm sorry I've no appointment –

RECEPTIONIST: Twenty past three Wednesday with Dr McClaren.

ELVA: I was hoping this afternoon –

RECEPTIONIST: Sorry, Wednesday's the earliest I can manage. (Phone. She lifts it.) Excuse me. Medical Centre, can I help you?

ELVA turns and goes. The RECEPTIONIST reaches for her appointments book. As ELVA goes out in the dark rainy afternoon we hear:

RECEPTIONIST: (OOV into phone) Can you manage 3.20 on Wednesday with Dr McClaren?

All very well if the intention is to portray the receptionist as unsympathetic but a problem if we have previously found her to be perceptive and warm hearted with a natural affinity for the young.

Sacrificing your character for sensation

Sacrificing a character on the altar of sensation is a major crime, most commonly done in soap operas. Perhaps a happily married woman suddenly goes berserk and starts having an affair with a character she has previously shown no interest in whatsoever. To understand why, we need to go back to a storyline meeting three months previously.

Producer, editors, storyliners and writers are fretting over what to do with Alice, who has not had a decent story for ages. This is a major crisis – not because the actress concerned is complaining night and day (nobody cares about that) but because she has been guaranteed 20 episodes (or at least payment for 20 episodes) and so far she has only been in three. The storyline meeting must find her a story! In the end somebody says: 'We've no story for George, either. Why don't they have an affair.' Everybody of sense at the meeting says it's impossible, Alice is 48 and president of the Mothers' Union, George is a 21-year-old rock singer. It simply would never happen! But the producer is a desperate woman (it's five minutes to opening time) so she says: 'Anything can happen in life, we mustn't be hidebound.' Alice has her pointless affair and her character is irrevocably altered.

It is easy to get a temporary sensation by making somebody behave oddly, but it does not work unless what happens genuinely springs from within the personality of the character concerned.

THE THOUGHT PROCESS

A drama ought to bring out character as a photographer's chemicals bring out the forms latent on the negative.

(William Archer)

The film *Three Into One Won't Go* opens with a middle-aged man driving his car. He comes across a very attractive girl thumbing a lift. He stops, some distance beyond her, opens the car door, and waits for her to come and jump in. When he looks back she is standing, hand on hip, waiting for him to back up to her. Unsmiling, he backs the car, and she gets in.

Not a word of dialogue has been spoken, but already we know of his middle-aged sexual frustration, and of her self-assurance and knowledge of the power she has over men of a certain age.

You cannot write for a character unless you know that character and understand what they are thinking at all times. When a character says something you always need to know why, because when an actor plays the part he must have a reason for what he is saying and doing. If you do not supply one, then the actor will have to find his own.

This sounds obvious – of course a writer knows what a character is thinking – but it is far from uncommon for a frustrated and simmering actor to corner a helpless writer after a read-through and say: 'I just cannot understand why I say this line on page 19: "Higgs deserves promotion if anybody does", when on page 5 I nodded in agreement when Jones said that Higgs was a brain-dead idle prat. Am I telling a complete lie? I mean, I can, of course, if that's what you intend.'

'Yes, that's it,' says the desperate writer, his mouth full of chicken vol-au-vent, but the actor continues remorse-lessly: 'But of course it totally affects the way I say the line, and if I'm lying why do I tell Sarah on page 24 that Higgs is the best thing that ever happened to the school?'

CHARACTER NAMES

When did you ever find a wicked Mary?

(BBC drama script editor)

A respected series writer had one failing. She could never think up a name for the new characters she had to introduce. She would ponder for hours, but her characters always ended up being called Robinson – usually Jim Robinson or Bill Robinson. A special effort might yield Robertson, and one day she even managed a Roberts. It was always left to the script editor to think up something different.

Names are strangely important. Given that in real life our personalities and names are connected in a totally arbitrary fashion, one ought to be able to produce six names for six characters and then shuffle them in a bag. But it does not work like that. See if you agree with the following.

- Hard names go with hard personalities; soft names with good-natured people.

- Working-class characters are called Bert and Maureen, toffs are called Simon and Emma.

- Young working-class characters are called Wayne and Sharon, young toffs are still called Simon and Emma.

- Working classes are surnamed Grice and Leech and Stott, toffs are surnamed Burlington-Smythe and Pomeroy and Beauchamp.

These are the clichés. But in real life, of course, the clichés are often true. You won't find many hereditary peers called Wayne or peeresses called Kylie, and if you shout 'Jeremy' or 'Henrietta' on a Toxteth housing estate you won't hear the patter of many tiny feet.

It is also true that the public has expectations from certain names, and the dramatist can use them as tools of his trade. A psychological study in America revealed that desirable names included Gregory and Craig; unpopular, undesirable names included Elmer, Hubert, Darrell and Horace. In Britain all the above names might be considered unappealing. A British report in the 1980s found that the public regard:

- John as trustworthy
- Robin as young

- Tony as sociable
- Agnes as old
- Ann as non-aggressive
- William as steady.

Names to help portray character

Some of the greatest writers have created names that contain within themselves the essence of the people they describe. David Copperfield's stepfather's sister was Miss Murdstone and the stolid carter was Barkis ('Barkis is willin' ').

Imagine the names changed about, with the hero David Barkis, the horrid stepfather's sister Miss Copperfield, and the carter murmuring 'Murdstone is willin' '.

The trick is to devise names that sound *appropriate* and at the same time avoid the obvious cliché. Jobbing gardeners should not be called Mr Potts – but neither should they be called Fossington-Fawcett (unless there is a deliberate irony, as when you call a pigman Lavender). Dashing, sexy heroes called Raymond Witson or Terry Stott or Kenneth Swindon are facing an uphill struggle, but so are Rik Steele and Jed Tempest.

Names to add colour

Names can be memorable (Dr Strangelove) or likeable and affectionate (Hawkeye and Trapper). The most important thing is that they should stand out (avoid too many characters called Smith and Brown and Tom and Fred) and should roll off the tongue in a satisfying way (Ena Sharples, Annie Walker).

And some to avoid
Avoid names that are similar – a Johnny and a Ronnie, a Mandy and a Sandy – in the same play.

SUMMARY

♦ Characters must have more than one characteristic.

♦ Avoid stereotypes.

♦ Do not force characters to behave stupidly in order to make a creaking plot work.

♦ Do not allow characters to behave out of character without reason or explanation.

♦ Remember that everything a character says or does reveals an aspect of their personality.

♦ Avoid cliché names.

Situation Comedy

Situation comedies – sitcoms – are commonly thought to be the hardest scripts of all to write. The problem – as one ITV Head of Comedy put it – is that whilst you can generally get some kind of broad agreement about the merits of a straight drama script, it is virtually impossible to find agreement over what is or is not funny. The first episode of *Jam and Jerusalem* was considered very funny by *Heat* magazine, but another critic said, 'This is like death'. The chemistry of the production is also vital and unpredictable. Sometimes scripts and actors seem brilliant, but the result, after rehearsal and recording, is dull, plodding and deadly. On the other hand a script thought desperately weak might suddenly take off when the cast and director get to work on it. It's a difficult area of writing, but the rewards are high if you can get it right. In this chapter we look at:

- the different types of situation comedy
- what the programme makers are looking for
- settings for sitcoms
- character in sitcoms
- structure in sitcoms
- to joke or not to joke?
- budgets
- hints for the new sitcom writer
- hit comedies.

THE DIFFERENT TYPES OF COMEDY

The most common reason for scripts being rejected – apart from them being simply not funny on any sort of level – is that they mix different styles, and thus fail at all of them. As a new writer, you need to be very clear from the beginning about the type of comedy you are writing.

1. Suspended disbelief

In situation comedies like *Blackadder* or *'Allo 'Allo* we happily suspend our disbelief. In other words we don't mind characters doing bizarre, illogical things or reacting to events in a way that would be unbelievable in rational human beings. When Baldrick spends a fortune on a turnip we don't say: 'This is ridiculous, no turnip could cost that much, and if it did surely Mr Blackadder would at least look surprised...' If we do say this sort of thing we are clearly humourless and our spouse will divorce us, and our pets will all seek new homes.

Comedies that incorporate the absurd are the most difficult to get right. All comedy involves a deviation from the norm, and if there are no rules of normal behaviour it is hard to get a laugh out of people deviating from them.

2. Comedy of wit and logic

In a programme like *Yes, Prime Minister* we are presented with a basically unbelievable situation: a not-very-bright prime minister willing to devote hours each day to being outwitted by one obviously manipulative civil servant. But once the unreality of the premise is accepted, the scripts are totally logical and the two characters completely rational and believable. *Fawlty*

Towers is the classic: supreme in that every story depends on the remorseless logic of the bizarre situations created.

3. Comedy of Life

From *Absolutely Fabulous* to *Phoenix Nights,* from *Coupling* to *The Office,* comedies about believable (if only just) people doing unusual, interesting or just well-observed things have been hugely successful. These comedies may differ in style but all of them are essentially about the way people live, about society today, about ambitions and hopes. We are not required to suspend our disbelief when we watch them – or at least, only a little bit. Most sitcoms fall into this category, and this is the area in which a new writer is most likely to succeed.

4. Broken comedy

This is sketch-type comedy, examples being *French and Saunders* and *Little Britain.*

WHAT THE PROGRAMME MAKERS ARE LOOKING FOR

Comedies that open with the reading of a will, or the winning of the lottery, are said to be clichés – but that doesn't mean you won't see both on screen in 12-months' time. At various times BBC 1 has asked for 'sophisticated, distinctive comedy which is adult in ambition and tone' for transmission after 9pm, and programmes that have 'inclusiveness and a sense of community' for pre-watershed showing. It is these comedies (e.g. *My Family, Only Fools and Horses, The Vicar of Dibley*), suitable for a family audience spanning three generations, that the BBC says are the hardest to find.

Otherwise, BBC 1 is not interested in 'laddish' comedies that follow the tradition of *Men Behaving Badly,* BBC 2 says it wants 'quick wit and clever observation to shine a light on favourite obsessions and pastimes' and Channel 4 has shown itself happiest when its comedies have something to say about society – hence *The Wilsons* which featured single parents and social workers – and with experimental shows that incubate writer-actor talent like *Ali G* and the all-female *Smack the Pony.*

There is a majority of women in charge of commissioning at the BBC these days and all those Janes and Kates and Sophies can't bear a series in which a group of lads sit around, talk about sport and take the piss out of each other.... The comedy buzzword at the BBC these days is 'uplifting'.

(BBC producer)

Both Channel 4 and BBC 3 target audiences in their twenties and thirties.

SETTINGS

Good sitcoms often take a very ordinary setting and then let the characters turn it upside down – suburbia in *One Foot in the Grave,* a seaside hotel in *Fawlty Towers.*

Zany, off-beat situations on the other hand are regarded as notoriously hard to make funny. 'A fish running an Internet café set on the dark side of Mars is not original but desperate,' says the BBC scathingly.

At the end of the day the setting is not as important as what you, the writer, do with it. 'Flat sharing' has for long been said to be an overworked and clichéd setting – but that didn't stop the BBC 2 hit *Gimme, Gimme, Gimme.*

CHARACTERS

Sitcom characters ought not to be too nice, says the BBC, and by nice they mean bland. Characters in comedy engage our interest because of their flaws, not because of their good nature. Captain Mainwaring and Victor Meldrew are likeable, of course, but it is the former's pomposity and the latter's frustration that makes us laugh. Most comedy characters have ordinary character-istics that are heightened. Stupid characters are extra stupid, snobby people are extra snobby. The golden rule is that *characters must be consistent.* In *Blackadder* Baldrick always has a cunning plan, Blackadder is always cynical, and the deeply, if engagingly, stupid character is always deeply and engagingly stupid.

Situation comedy is also very much about the **conflict** of characters within the situation you have set up. Conflict in sitcom can include:

◆ **Opposites** – *Friends* got much of its background comedy from an untidy person sharing a flat with an obsessionally tidy person; and a bloke confident with the opposite sex sharing a flat with a bloke who was insecure with the opposite sex.

◆ **Role reversal** – in *Absolutely Fabulous* Edina Monsoon is wild and irresponsible, while daughter Saffy is sensible and grown-up.

STRUCTURE

The structure of a sitcom is the same as that for any other kind of drama. (Crisis. Confusion. Resolution.) Typically in a sitcom, however, there will be a final twist to the end.

a) You set up a crisis.
b) The crisis deepens as your principal characters try – hilariously if possible – to resolve it.
c) They believe they have finally succeeded.
d) They suddenly find that they haven't.

The final stage might only last for 4 seconds – time for the ceiling to collapse, the studio audience to roar, and the signature tune to play loudly as we go chortling into the credits.

TO JOKE OR NOT TO JOKE?

The BBC in particular has an aversion to jokes and 'one-line gags'. You should not try to make every line a laugh, they say, severely, but should create humour out of characters reacting to comic situations with actions and dialogue. In other words, the rules of straight drama also apply to comedy. This does not mean you must avoid comic lines like Hancock's 'A pint? Ave you gone mad? That's very nearly an armful!' in *The Blood Donor*.

At the end of the day all you can do is write what you yourself believe to be funny. 'Do not simply try to match some mediocre show you saw on TV last night,' the BBC warns, probably fearing a thousand proposals based on *My Hero*.

If you can't come up with an idea just stick some kids in it, it never fails. 'My Son the Boss' – you work in a crazy company where your son is the boss, it's insane. 'Castaway Kids' – where you adopt some kids who were left on your doorstep. 'Kids in Space' – where you adopt some kids who were left on your doorstep by aliens.

(American writer Andy Kindler)

20 TOP TIPS FOR THE NEW SITCOM WRITER

1. Most successful sitcoms have only three or four central characters.

2. Those with a larger cast work best when there is a place where the characters can meet and interact without the need to explain what they are doing there. In *Dad's Army* and *The Vicar of Dibley* the characters meet naturally in the church hall, in *Phoenix Nights* they meet naturally at the Phoenix Club, in *The Office* they are in the office.

3. A high proportion of sitcoms explore aspects of the British character and the British way of life.

4. Most sitcoms are recorded before a live audience, and therefore have only three or four sets.

5. In sitcoms that are recorded before an audience, the action usually happens over a short period of time – this avoids changes in costume that slow down the recording.

6. Give yourself a theme – e.g. the recurrent theme of *Friends* is the nature of friendship; the theme of *Last*

of the Summer Wine is that you don't have to be young to be foolish; the theme of *Men Behaving Badly* is men behaving badly.

7.   Make sure that your theme – the premise of your situation – has ongoing comic possibilities.

8.   Few comic ideas can sustain half an hour. Consider having two or three stories running at once – they don't necessarily have to interweave, though it is regarded as neat if the outcome of one story alters or shapes the outcome of another.

9.   Don't rely on coincidence to make your plot work. The story should unfold the way it does because of the actions and reactions of your characters to a particular situation.

10.   As in other forms of drama, don't let your characters tell each other things they already know (and which they know they already know) just to make your story clear.

11.   Surprise and outwit your audience. The classic example provided by Charlie Chaplin was: A man walks along a street. The camera cuts to a banana skin on the pavement. The audience expect him to slip on it – but instead he carefully steps over it, looks back at it with a smile, and promptly falls down a manhole.

12.   Avoid spending the first dozen pages of your script introducing the characters and setting the scene. For some reason this almost always involves over-acting, feeble jokes, and forced humour. Start your episode

with a strong story that gives the actors something to act, and makes us want to know what happens next. Write two or three episodes, and then submit the best. It is surprising how little information is genuinely needed to introduce a situation and set of characters.

13. Humour has to be sustained. American sitcom producers aim to trigger a laugh every 13 seconds.

14. But don't force your humour. It must arise naturally from the situation you have skilfully created (in between your 13-second laughs).

15. Sitcom writing often works well as a joint effort – two writers exchanging ideas and rewriting each others' draft scripts.

16. Do not write for a specific star actor, even if you have an ideal actor in mind. The production companies want to see how you write original comedy for characters of your own creation.

17. Do not write a long explanation of why your idea is funny, and do not write long descriptions of your characters. Give a very brief synopsis (two or three lines if possible) of your story idea, short character notes if you must, then let your script itself do the work.

18. The BBC suggests that when you submit your script you tell them what writing experience you have had. Treat this advice with caution. It's fine to say you are new to television writing (they like to discover a star of tomorrow) but don't say that you have been writing

scripts and submitting them without success since *Dad's Army* was the best new sitcom of the year.

19. Go and watch a sitcom being made. For information on BBC sitcom recordings phone 020 8576 1227 or write to:
    BBC Audience Services
    PO Box 3000
    London WI2 7RJ

20. Take advantage of online comedy workshops. They are run from time to time by the BBC, Channel 4, and even by independent companies (see chapter 18).

HIT COMEDIES

For what it's worth, and to show what comedy afficionados want – which is not necessarily the same as what programme-makers want – in a 2004 BBC 2 poll to find the most popular British sitcoms, over 40% voted for either *Only Fools and Horses* or *Blackadder,* and for every viewer who voted for the critically-acclaimed *One Foot in the Grave* seven viewers voted for *The Vicar of Dibley.* The top ten were:

Only Fools and Horses
Blackadder
The Vicar of Dibley
Dad's Army
Fawlty Towers
Yes Minister
Porridge
Open All Hours
The Good Life
One Foot in the Grave

(10)

Presentation

HOW TO MAKE THE RIGHT IMPRESSION

The all-important moment will come when a script editor or professional reader opens your script at the first page – and instantly forms a judgement. This judgement will be based on the style and presentation of your work. It will be a superficial judgement and a work of quality will shine through the poorest layout. But it makes sense to give a good impression: the impression of a serious writer confident about his work.

PRESENTATION THAT LETS YOU DOWN

Avoid at all costs sending in scripts that are:

- written carelessly
- poorly laid out on the page
- lazily presented
- tired and travel-stained
- written for another medium (e.g. radio)
- professionally 'packaged'.

Careless scripts

Script editors are not impressed by scripts that are carelessly typed with obvious mistakes and characters muddled up:

JOHN
I love you now and I have always loved you.

SALLY
Conviction, John, conviction is what I want to hear.

SALLY
I love you and I have alwoys loved you, dammit!

SALLY
Somehow it still doesn't sund right.

As Sally cannot have three speeches one after another, it is, of course, easy to work out that the middle speech belongs to John. Typing errors are easily explained. But working this out slows up the reading of the script, interrupts the flow of the narrative, and reveals that the writer has not bothered to read his work through before posting it.

'I always write fast – once the idea comes to me I just have to get it down on paper, and once I've written it, that's it, I just can't look at it again.' So says the hopeful writer, presumably believing that the script editor will be impressed or at the very least indulgent.

The script editor will not be impressed or indulgent. The script editor will think: 'This is an amateur wasting my time.'

Poor layout on the page
Avoid layout that is confusing or unfamiliar, or makes it

hard to separate dialogue from studio directions. Do not write:

John 'Good Morning'
Jane 'Good morning, darling. What do you want for breakfast'
John 'Egg and bacon please.' John pauses then says 'On second thoughts I'll just have coffee.' Jane shakes her head.
Jane 'You and your silly diet'
John sits down and hides behind his copy of the paper. He is annoyed by Jane mentioning his weight again. I see the West Indies are all out for ninety five.
Jane 'You know I never read cricket.'

Scripts do arrive written like this, and the prejudice against them is considerable. The script editor assumes, reasonably, that if the writer cannot be bothered to consider the basic principles of script layout – or even to be consistent in the style he has chosen – then he has little chance of ever succeeding in the demanding, professional world of television.

Lazy presentation

A surprisingly large number of new writers use initials for the names of characters rather than spelling them out each time the character speaks. The writer tells us on the first page that his characters are called Henry and June and have two children called Kylie and Tom. In the script itself he writes:

H: I want everybody in the car in five minutes.

K: I can't find my cosie! Where's my cosie!
J: I haven't the foggiest idea, but I do know I told you to start looking for it three hours ago.
T: I've got mine. I always know where mine is.

Script editors hate this. They keep having to refer back to the front page to remind themselves who T is and who K is. This makes it hard for them to become absorbed in your work.

Tired and travel-stained script
Do not submit scripts that are:

◆ world-weary, crumpled and yellowing with age
◆ have comments on them from a previous submission.

Do not expect wonderful results from scripts that are creased and curly at the corners, decorated with ancient coffee stains, festooned with little messages like 'Ack 27/3/94' and with comments in the margins: 'Does not follow', 'Who is this character?', 'Weak dialogue' or even, showing the ultimate boredom, some previous script reader's shopping list. These are the signs of a well-travelled script that has seen the world and knows what it is to be rejected. It is a script that expects, even as the editor lifts it gingerly from her 'unsolicited' tray, to be rejected again. And it is.

A script must read clearly and easily as a piece of narrative; it must show its quality not only as a piece of writing, but as a piece of television writing.

(Arthur Swinson)

Scripts written for another medium

If you have had no luck with a radio play and decide to try it on television – fine. But make sure you adapt it first. There is no point in sending a radio play to a television company with the hopeful plea: 'Although this is written for radio, I now think it would be very good on television.' Few editors will bother to read it. You might just as well make a chair and try to sell it to somebody who wants a table.

If you do adapt a radio play, check it carefully before you send it off. All too often, around page six or seven, can be found the tell-tale sound direction: 'Fade up grams FX of storm at sea'.

It is also common for writers to adapt a play from television to radio, and still to leave in directions for cameras to pan, or cut, or zoom. Radio producers loathe this. They feel inferior enough already without people conning them into buying television drama's rejects.

Overkill presentation

Some writers go to endless trouble getting their script typed by a professional agency, often with the title printed via the magic of desktop publishing, and the result bound lavishly like a Hollywood studio script.

It seems heartless to say to a writer so obviously making an effort 'Don't bother' – but it is a mistake to spend too much time concentrating on presentation. Nobody is going to buy a script because it comes in a lavish presentation package. Many script editors will be actively put off.

There is a feeling that the script has already been 'processed' in some way, or that it is being dressed up smart to cover its inadequacies. The script editor, remember, is sustained by the hope that the next unsolicited script she reaches for will be a work of genius – a first offering by the Dennis Potter or Alan Plater of the future.

Somehow nobody expects genius to come in a glitzy, professional presentation.

> There is a perverse rule of thumb amongst editors and producers in British television that the more impeccably the script is presented, the duller the contents.
>
> (Eric Paice, writer)

PRESENTATION THAT HELPS YOU
Things to think about here are:

- page layout
- writing for the camera
- writing for the actor.

Page layout
Some new writers worry endlessly about layout. They know that television scripts wastefully use only half of the page, and that there is a mysterious professional code governing the use of CAPITAL letters for characters' names, and that colons and underlinings feature strangely, and that professional scripts are dotted with terse instructions demanding an MCU or a 2-SHOT or a PAN LEFT. (See Chapter 17, TV Talk.)

In fact, there is no fixed layout even among production scripts, which vary between the BBC and ITV companies and in small details often follow the personal whim of the production secretary. Certainly at the first stage of writing there are no vital formulae, and as you are not typing a studio script it is pointless to imitate one.

That said, it is common sense to conform to a layout that will be familiar to the script editor, and will be easy to read and to understand. Two of the basic rules are:

- always make a clear distinction between dialogue and description

- always leave a wide margin on the left-hand side of the page.

What you are trying to achieve is a simple, straightforward layout that will allow the reader or script editor to read your play effortlessly, gripped by your story, intrigued by your characters and savouring your excellent dialogue.

There are two basic layouts. They have one thing in common: they are easy to read, and they are familiar to script editors, readers and directors alike. (See Figures 1 and 2 on pages 113 and 114.)

The BBC also provides free script-layout software that you can download from *bbc.co.uk/writersroom*.

Writing for the camera
Should you indicate when you want a medium close up

(called an MCU)? or a two-shot? Or when you think the use of a crane shot or dolphin arm might be of artistic use? The answer is no, don't do any of these things unless they are vital to the telling of your story. Script editors find they get in the way, writers get bogged down in technicalities and end up thinking they have written a professional script just because it *looks* like a professional script.

It is not your job to write a camera script, it is your job to write a play.

At the same time you need to write with the camera in mind, and it is quite legitimate for you to indicate a camera move *if it is important to the telling of your story.*

Suppose you are writing a play about a doctor investigating the effect of a sinister new drug on blood cell structure. You want to open a scene with the screen filled with pictures of the drug molecules killing helpless blood cells, while a character tells excitedly of the discovery she has made.

INT. LABORATORY. DAY
The screen is filled with a computer simulation of ZYX cells attacking ABC cells. We hear DR WARD:

> WARD (OOV)
> They multiply at bloodheat, and within 2.4 seconds they begin to attack. They are deadly and they are irresistible. Your placebo, Professor Smith, is a killer.

<u>1. EXT. FRONT GARDEN OF CROSSLEY HOUSE. EARLY MORNING</u>

The front door opens and the family Rottweiler CONAN is let out into the garden.

> BOBBY (OOV)
> Go on, get out!

The front door closes. CONAN trots to the front gate and looks out. A dirty and rather old Ford escort is parked on the other side of the road.

<u>2. INT. UNMARKED POLICE CAR. EARLY MORNING</u>

DC ROBERTS, the passenger, stares across the road at CONAN.

> ROBERTS
> That's the best looking member of the family I've seen so far.

DC LAWLESS, the driver, peeps from behind his _Sun_.

> ROBERTS
> It looks almost intelligent, comparatively.

LAWLESS folds his paper and starts the car.

> LAWLESS
> Time for breakfast.

> ROBERTS
> It's the eyes, there's something behind them, that's what makes the difference.

<u>3. INT. BOBBY CROSSLEY'S BEDROOM. EARLY MORNING</u>

BOBBY is watching the car drive down the road.

> BOBBY
> Bastards.

Fig. 1. Script layout: style one.

47. EXT. CROSSLEYS FRONT GARDEN. NIGHT

TWO POLICE OFFICERS WEARING BLACK WITH BLACK
NYLON BALACLAVAS MOVE TOWARDS THE MOTORBIKE. THE
SECOND KEEPS WATCH AS THE FIRST STARTS TO FIX A
BLACK BOX TO THE UNDERSIDE OF THE BIKE.

48. EXT. CROSSLEYS BACK YARD. NIGHT

CONAN GETS UP AND LISTENS.

49. EXT. CROSSLEYS FRONT GARDEN. NIGHT

POLICEMAN ONE IS FIDDLING WITH THE BOX.

50. EXT. CROSSLEYS BACK YARD. NIGHT

CONAN MOVES TOWARDS THE FRONT OF THE HOUSE

51. EXT. CROSSLEYS FRONT GARDEN. NIGHT

CONAN APPEARS FROM THE BACK YARD. HE GROWLS

POLICEMAN TWO: (Whisper) Dog!

POLICEMAN ONE: Sodding hell, I thought
you said it was inside for the night.

CONAN GETS CLOSER AND MORE ANNOYED LOOKING.
POLICEMAN TWO GETS A LUMP OF PIPING FROM INSIDE
HIS LEATHER JACKET. CONAN LOOKS AT HIM.

POLICEMAN ONE: Do something about it.

POLICEMAN TWO CLUMPS CONAN OVER THE HEAD WITH THE
PIPING. CONAN WHIMPERS AND DROPS. POLICEMAN ONE
STARES DOWN.

POLICEMAN TWO: Get on with it,
they'll kill us now if they find us.

POLICEMAN ONE CONTINUES WITH HIS TASK. CONAN IS
BREATHING LIKE A DOG WITH A PROBLEM.

Fig. 2. Script layout: style two.

CUT TO: WARD and SMITH staring down at the screen. SMITH's face is expressionless.

WARD
You understand why I wanted you to come straight away. I'm sorry.

CUT TO: CU of SMITH staring down. From his POV we move slowly in again on the screen. Eerie theme music plays as we go closer and closer.

WARD (OOV)
Professor Smith? Are you all right?

In this illustration (OOV) indicates that Ward is speaking 'Out of Vision' and CUT TO indicates, as you would expect, that the camera cuts directly to WARD and SMITH. (We could have written PULL BACK instead of CUT TO, and this would have meant that the camera would slowly pull back from the screen to reveal the two characters staring down.) We then go to a CLOSE UP of SMITH before looking at the screen again from SMITH's POV ('Point of View') before the camera zooms slowly down again to a CLOSE UP of the battling blood cells.

These camera directions are quite acceptable as a way of telling your story. The director is unlikely to follow them: when the programme is made he will regard it as a point of honour to shoot the scene differently, but at least you will have shown your artistic intention. Camera directions commonly used by writers are as follows:

- POV – meaning we see something from a particular character's point of view.

- CLOSE UP (CU) – meaning the camera is close to something, generally somebody's face unless you indicate otherwise.

- PULL BACK – the camera is in close up and you want to pull back to show more.

- ZOOM IN – generally meaning that the camera moves quickly in on an object or person, although you can ask for a SLOW ZOOM.

- CUT TO – the camera cuts from one scene to another, or from one object to another. You can indicate that you want to cut from one person's face to another to show their reactions, but you are getting dangerously into the director's domain.

- OOV – the camera is showing something but we hear the voice of an actor who is speaking at the *same time* in the same scene.

- VO – the camera is showing a scene but we hear the 'Voice Over' of an actor who is not in the scene but might be narrating a story or recalling something in retrospect.

There are more television terms in Chapter 17, but generally speaking experienced writers leave pointing the camera to the person who's paid to point it: the director.

Writing for the actor
Actors have two major hates: not having a through line of

thought (much more about this in Chapter 7), and being told how they should feel at any particular moment.

> GEORGE
> (Playfully)
> I thought you said you hadn't bought a new dress.

> JOANNA
> (Angrily)
> I haven't bought a new dress, I've had this for ages.

> GEORGE
> (Tongue in cheek)
> That's impossible, it's the very latest fashion (cunningly devious) or perhaps my love, you would make any dress seem to be the latest fashion.

> JOANNA
> (Fondly)
> Oh George, oh do you really think so?

Some actors will tell you that 'mood directions' kill any chance they might have of building a scene during rehearsals, of developing moods themselves and finding their own moments of dramatic tension. They will tell you that if a script *needs* constant pointers as to mood then there is something wrong with it. They will say there is nothing worse than working on lines, creating a scene with a fellow actor, discovering from the text the thoughts and intentions of the character they are playing, and then suddenly finding that – for no reason they can fathom – they are supposed to say a line 'Whimsically' or 'Laughingly'.

The trouble is that not all actors are intelligent. There is a world of difference between:

JULIAN
(Acidly)
Well done. What a genius you are my dear.

and

JULIAN
(Warmly)
Well done. What a genius you are my dear.

And not every actor can be relied upon to know how you, the writer, intended it to be spoken. See how the above scene reads quite differently if we change the mood indicators.

GEORGE
(Sharply)
I thought you said you hadn't bought a new dress.

JOANNA
(Wearily)
I haven't bought a new dress, I've had this for ages.

GEORGE (Coldly) That's impossible, it's the very latest fashion (cutting) or perhaps, my love, you would make any dress seem to be the latest fashion.

JOANNA (Sarcastic) Oh George, oh do you really think so.

Writers cannot afford to trust actors entirely. Certainly not in soap operas and series where lines are being learned and performed very quickly. Many actors would not spot that a line was meant to be ironic if you hit them over the head with it, and no writer in his right mind trusts a television director to understand his script.

If you feel you need to indicate a mood at a given time, do so. If the script editor disagrees when she reads the script she will cross it out. Otherwise it will go through and, with luck, the actor will do what you want him to do.

From Script to Screen

TURNING A SCRIPT INTO A PROGRAMME

Here we look at how a long-running serial drama is made – from the initial idea, through the storyline stage, and through the different script stages and into production.

Jupiter Moon was a co-production made in 1990/1991 by an independent production company, Primetime Andromeda, for British Satellite Broadcasting and Axel Springer of Germany. One hundred and fifty episodes were recorded and are still being shown in over 30 countries worldwide, from the USA and Canada to satellite channels over Asia. Episodes are available on DVD from Amazon (UK) and in 2007 from Amazon (US) for region 1 players.

How writers are contacted for serial dramas

Jupiter Moon used several new writers. The script department worked to the following system which is common to most long-running serial dramas.

1. Script editors contact writers they have worked with in the past, and suggest that they read the programme's Guide for Writers and send in a trial script sample. Writers with a track record are paid to write a sample script, writers from another medium (i.e.

novels, radio) are sometimes expected to write a half-episode without a fee.

2. Agents (see page 244) are approached and told that the programme is looking for writers who can:

♦ write a strong narrative with good pacy dialogue

♦ write humour – not sitcom humour but the humour of human relationships

♦ have an interest in the particular programme's background, i.e. science fiction for *Jupiter Moon*.

3. New writers who telephone or write are usually asked to send in an example of their previous work. If this is interesting they will be asked to submit story ideas and/or write half a trial script (without fee). If this is greeted with enthusiasm they will be commissioned to write a single episode, and invited to their first script meeting.

Writers, therefore, come through personal contact, through agents, or by approaching the programme directly. Over the following pages (Figures 3–20) we see what happens next...

SUMMARY

♦ The writer is commissioned.

♦ The Guide for Writers describes what the programme is about and includes character breakdowns.

- Writers new to the programme are given guidance notes.

- The Storyline is distributed to writers after the storyline meeting.

- The script comes in from the writer.

- The script is sent to the specialist adviser – who adds his own notes and comments.

- The rehearsal script is typed up and distributed.

- The Props department goes through the script and makes a list of props needed for each scene.

- A requisition is made for food requirements.

- Special effects for the studio are ordered – anything from snow or fireworks to cobwebs and explosions.

- The director orders the graphics he will need.

- The PA breaks down the scenes and makes a brief note of what happens in each scene.

- The actors get their call times for wardrobe and make up.

- A studio script is marked with camera moves.

- The PA notes the running time of each scene – from the first rehearsal through to the Producer's Run, the studio, and the edit.

- After the studio the sound effects are dubbed on to the tape.

- Transmission details are sent to the broadcasting station.

Contract Number..003.....

AN AGREEMENT made the sixth   day of October 1989 between
PRIMETIME ANDROMEDA LIMITED whose registered office is 401, St. Johns
Street, London EC1V 4LH (hereinafter referred to as "Primetime
Andromeda") of the one part and JULIAN SPILSBURY of
                        Warwickshire hereinafter referred to as "The
Writer") of the other part.

WHEREBY IT IS AGREED as follows:-

Primetime Andromeda hereby commissions The Writer and The Writer accepts
the commission to write and deliver the scripts/script (hereinafter
referred to as "The Work") detailed in the table below in consideration
of the basic fees/fee payable in accordance with the table below and
subject to the attached terms and conditions.

DETAILS OF THE SCRIPTS/SCRIPT COMPRISING THE WORK

DESCRIPTION	PROGRAMME TITLE	APPROXIMATE DURATION	BASIC FEE
To write episodes 3, 6, 11, 12, 16, 23, & 24 for the series	"JUPITER MOON"	25 minute slot time	£ 1650.00 x7 £11550.00

DELIVERY DETAILS			TABLE OF PAYMENTS	
SCRIPT	DATE DUE	No.	WHEN DUE	AMOUNT
First and final drafts	between October and 18th December 1989	1	ON INDIVIDUAL COMMISSION	50%
		2.	ON ACCEPTANCE OF EACH SCRIPT	50%

The rewrite of each script
must be delivered within
SEVEN DAYS of notification
to The Writer by the Programme
Producer/Script Editor of a
requirement for said rewrite

All fees payable to The Writer hereunder shall be payable to Julian
Spilsbury whose receipt thereof shall be a complete and valid discharge
of Primetime Andromeda's liability

Fig. 3. The writer is commissioned – in this case an experienced writer is
commissioned for several episodes.

Introduction

JUPITER MOON is a serial drama about life in a space college in the year 2050. Although aimed at a young, intelligent audience it is not designed to be a "cult" space/science programme but to be a programme that will appeal to general viewers.

150 half hour episodes are being made between January 1990 and January 1991. Special effects and OB are being be filmed at Barrandov Studios, Prague, but the bulk of the programme is being recorded at Central Television Facilities, Birmingham.

JUPITER MOON is made by independent production company Primetime-Andromeda and has been shown on the Galaxy channel of British Satellite Broadcasting since March 26th, 1990.

The Idea

Columbus College in 2050AD is part of the University of Space, housed in the spaceship ILEA. It is used by the children of European scientists, administrators, and mining engineers working on the moons of Jupiter; and by undergraduates from Earth, Mars, SpaceStation and Moonstation.

The ILEA floats in permanent orbit over Callisto, the outermost of the Galilean moons. By the ship are the wharves and nuclear tugs of a vast space harbour.

Below, on the satellite itself, is the colony "Space City", with its liquid hydrogen plant, its hostel, spaceport, hospital, cafe/restaurant, nightclub and seedy bar.

JUPITER MOON is about the loves, passions, jealousies and ambitions of young people growing up in an alien but exciting environment.... how they mature as they learn to live with responsibility and cope with emotional relationships...

About the courage, fortitude, and occasional disillusion of men and women who have chosen to make new lives many million miles away from Earth... in particular the men and women working on "Daedalus 10" - a project to build man's first "starship" for a 12 year journey outside the Solar System.

Fig. 4. The **Guide for Writers** describes what the programme is about and includes character breakdowns.

IMPORTANT RULES FOR WRITERS

If you can stick to the following it helps us enormously at the production end.

Try not to have more than 29 scenes per episode (excluding special effect modelwork sequences)

Use only 12 characters per episode (if you need 13 talk to a script editor.)

Please use the script layout as per the sample at the end of this guide.

Please list the characters used, at the front of the script.

Each script should have between 44 and 47 <u>full</u> pages - if you like to go to a new page for a new scene make proper allowance for the blank sheets.

DON'T send in a genuine first draft. We need a script that you believe is ready to go into production. It should be properly polished, with tightly written stories, perceptive characterisation, and vivid, lively dialogue.

Please try to balance tense action stories with humorous themes and love/human interest themes.

Fig. 5. Writers new to the programme are also given guidance notes.

Episode 149: Part One (Cont)

Sara's Story

It's EVA 1 "space mobility" time for SARA and GABY. SARA has been desperately putting it off. She's happy to do the theory and go in the Zero Chamber - but not outside the ship! REBECCA says: "You've got to do it! What's the point in coming all the way to Jupiter System and never setting foot outside the ship?" Now SARA thinks it will have to be put off again because the Ilea is approaching Jupiter's magnetic field. She is quite cheery. Then DRUMMOND tracks her down. EVA space mobility is on!

GABY chats like an old campagner - she's been out on G33, she's been to Simpson Base! SARA is terrified. So, too, really, is GABY.

The Ship

VICTORIA joins DANIEL on the bridge. Petra announces: "Mercedes Page wishes everyone on the Ilea to know that her Engagement to Professor Charles Bonapart Brelan is cancelled, and invites all her friends to a celebration drink in the Club Galileo at 2100 hrs." DANIEL says: "Is it true about you and Brelan?". VICTORIA says: "Would you be surprised?" DANIEL: "You've always been the serious one." VICTORIA says: "I'm the one who couldn't stand change - I hated my Dad for making me come to Space, but I couldn't not come with him..."

"But you're the one going to Arial 9 - to swim in that ocean perhaps...walk a Mediterranian shore with no people, no pollution.. just sand and sea and sky" - "and little green men!"

A small surge in magnetic force. "Oi oi, better get them in." "Funny the forward opic sensors didn't react."

DRUMMOND in. Computer re-routing. The ship now entering the magnetopshere.... flashing lights.

The dead sentinels spring to life... not flashing amber but red. PETRA issues warning: Red Alert, Red Alert, override, override... and the ship heels as it goes to emergency burn. (Commercial Break)

Fig. 6. The **Storyline** is distributed to writers after the storyline meeting.

JIM reaches for his autosec. ANNA grabs her dressing gown
and staggers to the shower.

> JIM
> Petra, Red Spot Radio.

Music blares.

2. COMCEN

DRUMMOND just sitting down. On screen radar sweep with ALL
SYSTEMS ON AUTOMATIC over it in green.

> DRUMMOND
> Petra Systems and Met summary.

> PETRA
> Good Morning, Commander.

> DRUMMOND
> Good morning Petra.

> PETRA
> All shipboard systems nominal. We are on course
> to intercept with Hymalia in 17 hours 50.
> Metsat Ayola 9 reports ionised hydrogen and
> sulphur plumes (<u>Doug help!!!</u>)

REBECCA IN

> REBECCA
> Why does my heart sink when metsats go on about
> sulphur plumes.

> DRUMMOND
> Scale four. We won't even notice. What are you
> doing up?

> REBECCA
> Petra what woke me up at 0500 hours?

Fig. 7. The script comes in from the writer – this is the generally accepted layout.

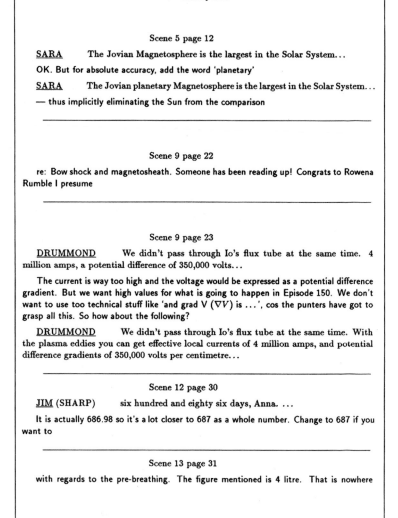

JUPITER MOON — EPISODE 149

6th January 1991

Scene 5 page 12

<u>SARA</u>   The Jovian Magnetosphere is the largest in the Solar System...

OK. But for absolute accuracy, add the word 'planetary'

<u>SARA</u>   The Jovian planetary Magnetosphere is the largest in the Solar System...

— thus implicitly eliminating the Sun from the comparison

Scene 9 page 22

re: Bow shock and magnetosheath. Someone has been reading up! Congrats to Rowena Rumble I presume

---

Scene 9 page 23

<u>DRUMMOND</u>   We didn't pass through Io's flux tube at the same time. 4 million amps, a potential difference of 350,000 volts...

The current is way too high and the voltage would be expressed as a potential difference gradient. But we want high values for what is going to happen in Episode 150. We don't want to use too technical stuff like 'and grad V (∇V) is ...', cos the punters have got to grasp all this. So how about the following?

<u>DRUMMOND</u>   We didn't pass through Io's flux tube at the same time. With the plasma eddies you can get effective local currents of 4 million amps, and potential difference gradients of 350,000 volts per centimetre...

Scene 12 page 30

<u>JIM</u> (SHARP)   six hundred and eighty six days, Anna. ....

It is actually 686.98 so it's a lot closer to 687 as a whole number. Change to 687 if you want to

---

Scene 13 page 31

with regards to the pre-breathing. The figure mentioned is 4 litre. That is nowhere

Fig. 8. The script is sent to the scientific adviser – who adds his own notes and comments.

JUPITER MOON
EPISODE ONE HUNDRED & FORTY NINE

ANDROMEDA

WEEK 5	DIRECTOR: David Dunn
EPISODE 149	PA: Fiona Napier
	PRODUCER: William Smethurst
STUDIO	ASSOCIATE PRODUCER: Jane Fallon
29TH, 30TH, 31ST JANUARY	WRITER: Rowena Rumble
	POST PRODUCTION EDITOR: Diane Culverhouse
	SCRIPT EDITOR: Jane Fallon

CAST [in order of appearance]

* PROFESSOR BRELAN......................... RICHARD DERRINGTON
  MERCEDES PAGE............................ ANNA CHANCELLOR
  PETRA (VO)............................... CHARLOTTE MARTIN
  PAUL FITZROY DRUMMOND.................... RICHARD HAINSWORTH
  REBECCA HARVEY.......................... ALISON DOWLING
  ANNA BEGANI............................. ANNA PERNICCI
  DANIEL WETHERBY......................... DANIEL BEALES
  VICTORIA FROBISHER...................... NICOLA WRIGHT
  FIONA McBRIDE.......................... LUCY BENJAMIN
  SARA ROBBINS........................... KAREN MURDEN
  GABRIELLA TANZI........................ FAY MASTERSON
  JIM HAWKINS............................ JIM SHEPLEY

Fig.9. The rehearsal script is typed up and distributed.

SCENE 149.2 INT DAY 2 0730
SET COMCEN

DRUMMOND:	Richard H
PETRA (VO):	Charlotte
REBECCA:	Alison
ANNA (ON SCREEN):	Anna P
MERCEDES (ON SCREEN):	Anna C

DRUMMOND JUST SITTING DOWN. ON
SCREEN RADAR SWEEP WITH 'ALL SYSTEMS
ON AUTOMATIC' OVER IT IN GREEN.

DRUMMOND: Petra, Systems and Met
summary.

PETRA (VO):   Good morning,
Commander.

DRUMMOND: (WEARY TOLERANCE)
Good morning Petra.

PETRA (VO):   All shipboard systems
nominal. We are on course to
intercept Hymalia in 17 hours 50.
Metsat Ayola 9 reports ionised
hydrogen and sulphur plumes scale 4
zero zero in Io flux tube, intercept
T minus 8 hours forty.

REBECCA IN.

REBECCA: Why does my heart sink
when metsats go on about sulphur
plumes.

DRUMMOND: Scale four. We won't
even notice. What are you doing up?

4

Fig. 10. Layout of the rehearsal script.

TO: ALAN BARRETT   cc: Setting Office x 2
                                                Design x 2
FROM: PETER COTTON   FM & AFM's
                                                Props Stores
DATE: 7th December 1990   PA
                                                Director

JUPITER MOON: PROPS REQUIREMENTS: EPISODES 136/137/138

EPISODE 136 (Studio Date): 18th December 1990

SC	SET	PROPS
1	STORAGE ROOM	N/P
2	EXT ILEA	N/P
3	COMCEN	Breakfast ?
4	LONG CORRIDOR	Tim's jacket with food in pockets
5	STORAGE ROOM	Mushroom Quiche ?
6	GANTRY 2 LOBBY	Coffee, Finbow's glasses
7	COMCEN	Finbow's glasses
8	LAB 5	Files, papers etc
9	COMMON ROOM	Breakfast, autosec - Jim
10	LIFT	N/P
11	LECTURE THEATRE	Files, papers etc
12	EXT ILEA	N/P

Fig. 11. The Props department goes through the script and makes a list of props needed for each scene.

M E M O R A N D U M

TO: DAVID WRIGHT - CATERING MANAGER   cc: Setting Office x 5
                                                  Design x 2
FROM: PETER COTTON   FM + AFM's
                                                   P A
DATE: 12 DECEMBER 1990   Director

JUPITER MOON: PROP FOOD REQUIREMENTS: EPISODES 136/137/138

TUESDAY 18 DECEMBER 1990

3 Doz. Canapes (some to be for a vegetarian)
18 Grilled Mock Halibut Steaks (To look like Salmon)
Tarragon + Cream Sauce (Must be seperate not on fish)
18 Portions of Braised Fennel
18 Portions of Stuffed Aubergines (Vegetarian Stuffing)
48 Profiteroles (Golf Ball Size) (Orange Sauce Separate- with bits of
orange peel in it)
24 Jam Packs
24 Butter Packs

****

WEDNESDAY 19 DECEMBER 1990

Nothing Required

****

THURSDAY 20 DECEMBER 1990

Ass. Salad for 10 people

****

Many thanks

Fig. 12. A requisition is made for food requirements.

CENTRAL — Originator

SPECIAL EFFECTS — SPECIALITY PROPS REQUIREMENTS

Date Issued 16.12.90 Production a JUPITER MOON Prod No. 8500/137 Date Req 19.12.90 P.A. SHAN DUCKETT Ext. 4006

RAIN [C.M.]	SNOW—Falling —Static [C.M. S.M.]	WIND [C.M. S.M.]	FOG [E.S. L.W.]	SMOKE [C.M. E.S. L.W.] 137.18 – Dome 137.24 – Dome	STEAM [C.M. E.S. L.W.]
COBWEBS [C.M.]	B.P.—Still —Moving [C.M. S.M. Proj.]	HOUSE APPLIANCES Elec. Prac. [C.M. S.M. Proj.]	HOUSE APPLIANCES Gas—prac. [E.S. S.M. L.W.]	DROP BOXES [C.M. S.M.]	LAMPS—prac. [S.M. E.S. L.W.]
WATER—tanks [S.M. C.M.]	WATER—Baths/ Showers [S.M. C.M.]	WATER—Baths/ Sinks [C.M.] Poss.prac hand basin t.b.c 137.1 & 137.3	LAB EFFECTS [C.M.]	DRY ICE MACHINE [C.M.]	FIRES—Log [C.M.]
FIRES—Coal [C.M.]	CANDLES—prac. or not [C.M.]	EXPLOSIONS [S.M.]	FLAME EFFECTS [C.M. E.S. L.W.]	MACHINE GUN EFFECTS [C.M. E.S. L.W.]	FIREWORKS [C.M. E.S. L.W.]
ANIMATED PROPS [C.M.]	MAGIC TRICKS/ EFFECTS [C.M.]	FIRE EXTINGUISHERS —prac. [C.M. S.M.]	GUNS—practical Non-prac. [C.M. S.M.]	BALLOON NETS [C.M. S.M.]	REVOLVES Turntables [E.S. S.M. L.W.]

1. Fill in relevant section giving brief details about effect required.
2. If the effect you require is not specified please use the blank sections.

Fig. 13. Special effects for the studio are ordered – anything from snow or fireworks to cobwebs and explosions.

GRAPHICS SPFX

DIRECTOR HENRY FOSTER

P.A.

EPISODE: 136

EPISODES 136-138

STUDIO 18 - 20 Dec

EDIT 7 - 9 Jan.

SCENE	PAGE	SPFX DESCRIPTION	NEW/ EXISTS	GRAPHICS ACTION REQUIRED	TAPE NO.	TIMECODE
2	8	EXT: SUNRISE OVER GANYMEDE	EXISTS	NO	459	53.60
3	9	CONCEN: General	EXISTS	NO		
7	17	DITTO	....	....		
8	19	LAB 5: DRUMMOND WORKING: Oort cloud?	NEW	YES		
11	26	LECT. THEATRE: Graphics as per page.	NEW	YES		
12	28	EXT: ILEA IN TRANSIT: DAY	EXISTS	NO	757	01.00 - 01.39
13	29	DOME?				
14	32	CONCEN: Scan of ship especially central storage bay hangar. Then hologram of Tim comes up. _General scan of ship:_	EXISTS?		768	03.25.

Fig. 14. The director orders the graphics he will need.

SCENE	PAGE	ARTISTES	D/N	OB/ STUDIO	NOTES
136.8	22 to 24	INT LAB 5 REBECCA DRUMMOND MERCEDES	DAY 1 0900		Mercedes decides to invite Drummond a Rebecca to the dinner party
136.9	25 to 29	INT COMMON ROOM JIM SARA BRELAN MERCEDES	DAY 1 0905		Brelan asks Jim to the prepare the meal for the party but is surprised when Merc tells him it is for 6 peop
136.10	30 to 31	INT LIFT MERCEDES BRELAN	DAY 1 0907		Mercedes asks Brelan if he minds her invite Drummond & Rebecca to the party
136.11	32 to 34	INT LECTURE THEATRE JIM DANIEL SARA NS STUDENTS 'MODULE ONE STUDENTS	DAY 1 0930		Daniel is not interested in helping with the party & Jim decides not to move into Cabin 3 with him
136.12	35 to 35	EXT EXT ILEA	DAY 1 1029		EXT
136.13	36 to 39	INT DOME JIM SARA <s>AND PLAYERS COST</s>	DAY 2 1030		Jim decides what to cook for the d party & Sara decides she will help with the serving
136.14	40 to 41	INT COMCEN NATASHA PETRA (VO) TIM (HOLO)	DAY 1 1045		Tim is discovered in the central storag bay hangar - Natasha is annoyed
			End of PART		
136.15	42 to 44	INT COMMON ROOM JIM SARA	DAY 1 1930		Jim & Sara start to prepare the meal - Sara is having problem Jim gets annoyed
136.16	45 to 46	INT BRELAN'S SUITE BRELAN MERCEDES	DAY 1 1944		Brelan gets the drinks ready - Mercedes arrives & Brelan sends her away to get changed

Fig. 15. The PA breaks down the scenes and makes a brief note of what happens in each scene.

EPISODES 148/149/150

VTR: TUESDAY 29TH JANUARY, 1991

ARTISTE	CHARACTER	WARDROBE	MAKE UP	ON SET
NICOLA WRIGHT	VICTORIA	0800	0830	0900
RICHARD DERRINGTON	BRELAN	0830	0845	0900
JANNA STRIEBECK	TRANQUILITY	0800	0830	0915
ANNA CHANCELLOR	MERCEDES	0800	0830	0930
ALISON DOWLING	REBECCA	0845	0915	1000
CHRISTOPHER SIMON	CHRISTOPHE	0930	0945	1000
FAY MASTERSON	GABRIELLA	0915	0945	1015
JIM SHEPLEY	JIM	0930	0945	1015
LUCY BENJAMIN	FIONA	1000	1030	1100
KAREN MURDEN	SARA	1000	1030	1100
RICHARD HAINSWORTH	DRUMMOND	1045	1100	1115
DANIEL BEALES	DANIEL	1145	1200	1215
ANNA PERNICCI	ANNA	1415	1445	1530

Fig. 16. The actors get their call times for wardrobe and make up.

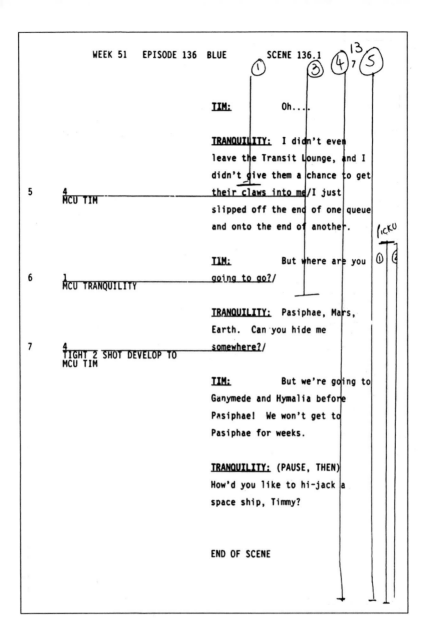

TIM: Oh....

TRANQUILITY: I didn't even leave the Transit Lounge, and I didn't give them a chance to get their claws into me/I just slipped off the end of one queue and onto the end of another.

5 4
MCU TIM

TIM: But where are you going to go?/

6 1
MCU TRANQUILITY

TRANQUILITY: Pasiphae, Mars, Earth. Can you hide me somewhere?/

7 4
TIGHT 2 SHOT DEVELOP TO
MCU TIM

TIM: But we're going to Ganymede and Hymalia before Pasiphae! We won't get to Pasiphae for weeks.

TRANQUILITY: (PAUSE, THEN) How'd you like to hi-jack a space ship, Timmy?

END OF SCENE

Fig. 17. A studio script marked with camera moves.

from   J.H.Parker.

to   H.Foster,S.Duckett,Sound Dubbing.

date   20/12/90

<u>JUPITER MOON DUBBING NOTES EPISODES 136-138.</u>

Episode 136.

Sc 5   Door open.

Sc 8   Door open and close.

Sc 10   Lift arrive,stop and depart.

Sc 16   Door open and close.

Sc 18   Door open and close.

Sc 20   Composed of different passes and pickups.
             Start of sequence   Roll 203/28-19
             WT trolley   Roll 203/44-16
             WT crockery breaking Roll 203/44-38

Sc 22   Composed of different passes and pickups.
             Start of sequence Roll 203/37-48

Sc 26   Doors open and close.

Sc 29A   Door open and close X 2.

Sc 31   Door open and close X 2.
             Door buzz on light cue.
             WT Daniel's "Lights."   Roll 204/45-04

Episode 137.

Sc 1   Door open and close.
             Music "Africa".

Sc 2   Add FX of two cups of coffee being poured.

Sc 3   Door open and close.
             Music "Africa".

Sc 10   Lift arrive.

                                       (Continued)

Fig. 18. The PA notes the running time of each scene – from the first rehearsal through to the producer's Run, the studio, and the edit.

SCENE	READ		FRI	SAT PROD RUN	MON	XTR...	EDIT
REPRISE	0025	0025	0025	0025	0025	0058 0058	
OPENING TITLES	0035	0100	0035	0100	0035	0036 0134	
CABIN 3	0050	0150	0040 0140	0035	0040	0002 0201	
COMCEN	0035	0225	0040 0220	0040 0215	0040 0215	0036 0237	
CABIN 3	0030	0255	0030 0250	0030 0245	0035 0240	0030 0307	
COMCEN	0125	0420	0120 0410	0120 0405	0130 0410	0026 0333	
GANTRY & LOBBY	0045	0505	0035 0445	0035 0440	0035 0445	0037 0410	
COMMON ROOM	0050	0555	0045 0530	0045 0525	0045 0530	0045 0455	
COMCEN R	0055	0650	0100 0630	0100 0625	0040 0550	0020 0515	
CABIN 3	0115	0805	0100 0730	0100 0725	0115 0705	0053 0608	
CABIN 1	0010	0815	0010 0740	0010 0735	0010 0715	0010 0618	
GYM	0135	0950	0135 0915	0130 0905	0140 0855	OUT →	
CABIN 1	0055	1045	0115 1030	0125 1030	0110 1005	0040 0405	
CABIN CORRIDOR	0035	1120	0030 1100	0030 1100	0030 1035	0036 0741	
CABIN 1	0035	1155	0035 1135	0040 1140	___ 1120	0048 0829	
CABIN 3	0105	1300	0140 1315	0135 1315	0135 1255	0131 1001	
COMCEN	0045	1345	0045 1400	0045 1410	0120 1415	0105 1126	
CABIN 1	0040	1425	0040 1440	0050 1450	0100 1515	0102 1228	
END PART ONE	0005	1430	0005 1445	0005 1455	0005 1520	0003 1231	
	PT 1 1430	PT 1 1445	PT 1 1445	PT 1 1455	Part 1 1520	Part 1 1231	
	PT 2 1027	PT 2 1117	PT 2 1117	PT 2 1100	Part 2 1110	Part 2 1154	
TOTAL	TOTAL	TOTAL	TOTAL	TOTAL	TOTAL	TOTAL	

Fig. 19. After the studio the sound effects are dubbed onto the tape.

TRANSMISSION INFORMATION

IF PROGRAMME IS DELIVERED ON DAY OF TRANSMISSION **PLEASE**
FAX TOP SHEET (THIS PAGE (1)) TO PRESENTATION DEPT. FAX. NO.: 627 6565
FAX PAGES 2 AND 3 (COMMERCIAL REFERENCES TO AIR TIME SALES Fax. NO.: 627 6256
HARD COPY OF PAGES 1-12 TO PROGRAMME SERVICES DEPT. FAX NO.: 627 6556

PROGRAMME TITLE: JUPITER MOON.
BSB PROG. NO: 000 12580
SERIES TITLE: JUPITER MOON   EP 136 OF
FIRST TX DATE/TIME:_____ CHANNEL:_____
IS PROGRAMME CONTINUOUS OR DISCONTINUOUS? DISCONTINUOUS
ARE THERE END/BEGINNING OF PART CAPTIONS? YES
PLEASE INDICATE BELOW ACTUAL OR ADVISORY BREAK POINTS.
Pt 1. TC IN: 00:03:00:00 TC OUT: 00:14:13:06 DURATION: 11'.13"
        CUE IN:_____
        CUE OUT:_____
Pt 2. TC IN: 00:16:00:00 TC OUT: 00:28:51:00 DURATION: 12'.51
        CUE IN:_____
        CUE OUT:_____ TOTAL
Pt 3. TC IN:___:___:___:___ TC OUT:___:___:___:___ DURATION: 24'.04"
        CUE IN:_____
        CUE OUT:_____
(PLEASE CONTINUE MORE PARTS ON SEPARATE SHEET)
TOTAL PROGRAMME DURATION (min:sec): 24:04.
FIRST END CREDIT: TIMOTHY SHAW (ANDREW READ)   AT TC: 00.28.02.15
LAST END CREDIT: PRIMETIME ANDROMEDA   AT TC: 00.28.51.00
DOES PROG CONTINUE AFTER LAST END CREDIT? NO
ATTACH ANY CONTACT NUMBERS OR ADDRESSES MENTIONED IN PROGRAMME. PLEASE ADVISE OF ANY
FACTORS AFFECTING TRANSMISSION OF PROG., (eg. Mute sections, Periods of black, Contrived breakdowns,
Deliberate distortion of sound or vision)

PRODUCTION COMPANY:_____ TEL:_____
ADDRESS:_____ FAX:_____

PRODUCER/DIRECTOR_____ HOME TEL:_____
ADDRESS:_____

PRODUCTION COMPANY'S TAPE NO: 7195P30

PLEASE RETURN ALL THESE COPIES TO B.S.B., THE MARCOPOLO BUILDING, QUEENSTOWN ROAD, LONDON SW8 4NQ.

Fig. 20. Transmission details are sent to the broadcasting station.

The Difficult Markets

WHICH ARE THE MOST DIFFICULT AREAS TO GET INTO?

The hardest markets for new writers are:

◆ single plays
◆ serials
◆ adaptations.

SINGLE PLAYS

These are the prestige dramas that aspire to say something significant about the world in which we live. Through the single television play some of the best writers in Britain have been discovered and nurtured. Playwrights like David Edgar, David Hare, David Rudkin (David is clearly a helpful name in television drama) have written some of their most important work for the single television slot.

Today, sadly, few writers are discovered and nurtured through one-off drama, and this has become one of the most difficult slots for the beginner. There are two reasons for this. Firstly, broadcasters have moved more and more to long-running series dramas that can build a mass audience. Secondly, the cost of making the single play has risen sharply because of the visual expectations of viewers.

What viewers look for

When Sydney Newman was producing *Armchair Theatre* on ITV the single drama was both popular viewing and cheap to make. Writers nurtured on the theatrical tradition wrote intelligent plays in which the action was contained in one or two studio sets, and which had few characters.

Today viewers expect more. They expect single plays to be shot on film, they expect gloss and colour and excitement on the screen, they expect to be visually as well as mentally entertained. The cost of the single-play drama shot on film is now well over a million pounds per hour. This is the most expensive television there is.

Our focus on TWO .... is to create drama events of immense scale and impact. Broad in cultural and geographical appeal, we are looking for 1 or 2 very big ideas a year, that will take audiences to places that drama has never taken them before.

(BBC Commissioning Guide)

The BBC and Channel 4 now call single plays, or plays shown over two nights, 'event drama', by which they mean drama that will be sensational enough, either in its subject matter (e.g. Channel 4's *Sex Traffic*, a multi-strand story about the sex industry filmed in five different countries) or in its star casting, to be widely noticed and commented on by newspapers and magazines. These 'event dramas' will certainly be international co-productions. Well-crafted single plays, dealing with domestic British issues, are still made by ITV. But there are fewer slots than in the past, and it is increasingly rare for these precious, prestigious, incredibly expensive dramas to be given over to the new writer. BBC2's hugely ambitious *Decades* was entirely commissioned before it was even announced.

Single plays are normally written by:

♦ Television writers with a track record. A writer puts forward an idea to a producer or independent production company, and is then commissioned to write a script.

♦ Writers from other media – journalism, literature – who already have a high (or at least interesting) reputation.

Even among prestigious writers more scripts are commissioned (such is the power of a good lunch and a persuasive top literary agent in a Charlotte Street restaurant) than there are slots available. When a new writers sends in an unsolicited script, therefore, he is likely to be competing for the sole remaining slot of the year against a script by an established writer that has already cost the BBC or Channel 4 several thousands of pounds.

So should a new writer bother writing a one-off play?

The answer is most definitely YES – and for the following reasons.

1. As was said in **How to Succeed** on page 6 a single play of your own devising is your *curriculum vitae* – your claim to be taken seriously. In the one-off 60-minute or 90-minute play you are creating your own world,

with your own characters, in your own style. You writing is likely to be at its best and its mo convincing.

2. There is the possibility that you will achieve somethin wonderful, and that your play will be read by producer who likes it and has the opportunity to put on. There is also the possibility that your play will I read and remembered later.

    It does happen. A completely unknown writer sent 90-minute film script to BBC Pebble Mill. It was like by a script editor who pushed it for production, b without success. Months later a production collapse and there was a search for a replacement. Th unknown writer – who had given up hope – receive a phone called saying her play would start pr production the following week, with Jane Lapotai in the lead role.

3. There is a good chance that if your play shows genuin talent you will be considered as a writer for anoth slot. Most writers on soap operas and series drama first attracted attention to their skills by submittin single plays.

Step by step for the new writer

◆ Unless you have a story that needs 90 minutes, wri for a 60-minute slot. There are more of these availab than 75- or 90-minute slots.

◆ On no account write for longer than 90 minutes.

◆ For the BBC and Channel 4 your idea needs to be big and bold and say something controversial, fascinating, or frightening, about contemporary life or society.

◆ ITV will be interested in family drama, or comedy drama, or social drama – but you need to bring to it a new slant, a new voice.

◆ Do not write period drama, because it is very expensive and single plays almost always concern themselves with life today.

◆ If you have specialist knowledge use it. Try to take us into a world that you know better than anyone else. If you have given birth to a baby and spent a year under the Pacific in a nuclear submarine you have at least two experiences that put you one up on the majority of TV dramatists.

◆ Write for a reasonably small cast (i.e. don't demand hundreds of participating extras) and avoid elaborate and expensive set-ups (i.e. don't demand that filming takes place at a hot air balloon rally at the South Pole) because producers might be looking for a lower-cost drama (in BBC terms perhaps £700,000 an hour rather than £1,000,000) to compensate for the high budget 'events' to which they have previously committed themselves.

◆ Write for film, with outside locations. Few if any single dramas are now shot in the studio.

◆ Try to think of interesting but low-cost locations: fairgrounds give colour and visual interest, and fairgrounds are not too difficult for the production to

find. Canal barges, the seaside, a hot air balloon ral
that *isn't* at the South Pole – these are locations that g
us out and about without costing the production
fortune. Try to think of locations that are cheap b
different!

SERIALS

A serial tells an on-going story and has a set number
episodes. Often serials are in four parts, or six parts, bu
this is a matter of fashion and changes year by yea
Serials include original dramas and adaptations
popular novels and classics.

There have traditionally been few opportunities here fo
the new writer. A drama department might make three
four serials a year, and will have a huge choice
materials and writers to select from. If it is rare fo
television to commission a new writer for a one-off play,
is almost unheard of to commission four or six hours
drama from somebody with no track record. BBC1 ha
said that it is looking for 'signature writers' which
another way of saying big names.

But television is constantly changing, and if you have
strong idea for a serial – say a thriller, or comedy dram
in four or six episodes – then you should go for it. Chann
4 and BBC 2 are always asking for ideas for late-nigh
low cost drama, and BBC 1 says it is interested in origin
drama ideas for 'post-peak' (around 10pm) slots that 'ca
be realised at a much lower cost through innovation and
or experiment'. What they mean by innovation an
experiment is unclear, unless they are suggesting the use

puppets, but there must be opportunities here for the new writer.

Step by step for the new writer

- Write an opening episode and a synopsis of the other episodes. Each synopsis should be at the most two pages long (reasonably spaced out and easy to read). Don't break your synopses down into scenes but tell the broad sweep of the story, showing that each episode has an exciting opening, strong development, and a cliff-hanger climax.

- Your best chance is to write for a low budget slot (for the production team this means around £450,000 for a 50-minute episode). Both Channel 4 and BBC 2 would be very, very happy if a strong well-scripted story was offered that they could make for £350,000 an episode. BBC2 has said that it has late night opportunities for those who embrace 'new technology and/or ways of working' which is yet another way of saying low cost. From a writer's point of view: make it a small cast with no car chases and few locations.

- As with the one-off single drama, give us something fresh and original. Script editors yearn for something vivid and exciting, that hasn't been done before.

ADAPTATIONS

Whether it be classic period adaptations like *Bleak House* or *Sense and Sensibility*, or a modern novel like *The History Man*, the television company embarking on a multi-million pound project is going to look for a writer of experience to adapt the original material. This is the most difficult market to get into.

Like most writers, though, you probably have a favouri book (let us call it *Pigs Might Fly*) which you belie would make a terrific television serial. It is just possib that you could offer your adaptation at exactly the rig time to a producer who a) is also passionately fond *Pigs Might Fly*, b) thinks you have done a terrif adaptation and c) has the muscle to get both the boc and you accepted by the network scheduler.

In the case of classic novels, you should write a synopsis the dramatic ground you would cover in each episode, an then write the first episode as an example of your work

With modern novels, it is a more interesting situation. T work is in copyright, and the television rights could easi have been sold elsewhere. You might spend weeks toilir on an adaptation only to find that another writer is doir the same – but under commission for a televisic company that has taken out an option on the book.

If you believe your skills lie in the field of adaptation, d not be put off trying, but check the following before yc start:

◆ Has the novel been done on television before, and if a how long ago was it? Generally speaking televisic does not worry about things previously done in blac and white.

◆ Are the television rights in the book available? T publisher will gave you the name of the writer's agen who will have this information.

- If the rights are available, will the writer agree to you adapting their work? Many writers, sensibly, are careful about who they allow to adapt their novels.

- If the rights are available, and the writer has no objection to you as adaptor, all you have to do is find a television company interested in putting it on.

Can I acquire rights in a book myself?

Yes, of course – again if the writer is willing to give you an option. Independent producers often take out options on books and then try to sell the idea to a television company.

In the general run of things an option on a book is not expensive. You can secure an option for twelve months for a few hundred pounds. This gives you the exclusive right to make a television programme out of the book during the period of the option. As you would expect, to option a best seller or a book by a very successful author will be much more expensive.

Of course you might be lucky enough to buy the rights in a book just before it becomes an international best seller – and then have the satisfaction of having the BBC, ITV and Channel 4 desperate to get hold of it, and happy to commission you as the adaptor. Everybody can dream....

(13)

Programmes Looking for Writers

WHICH ARE THE BEST PROGRAMMES TO TRY?

The television slots that offer the most opportunity to new writers are:

- ◆ series dramas
- ◆ short plays
- ◆ children's drama
- ◆ situation comedy.

(Soap operas are covered separately in the next chapter.)

SERIES DRAMAS

Series dramas generally run for an hour, and there are a lot of them on television. In a series we have an established situation and established central characters, but each week we have a new story that also brings in its own characters.

A series will sometimes have only six or seven episodes, but more often it will have a magnificent 13, and will run for a quarter of the year.

Programme schedulers love series dramas because they build up an audience week by week. New writers ought to love them because of the opportunity they present.

How to write for a series

In its first run a series might have been written by a picked team of three or four writers (usually including the series devisor), but when a further series is planned the script editors instantly start to look around for fresh blood. Thirteen scripts might not seem too difficult to find, but to get them 40 or 50 storylines might be considered, and many of those will be put through two or three drafts. Then, perhaps 15 scripts will be commissioned – and when the first five come in and are hopeless the editor will panic and commission a whole lot more.

This may seem profligate, as fees can be over £6,000 for a 60-minute slot and the first half payment (50 per cent up front) will be paid whether the script is accepted or not. Consider, though, that each programme is going to cost up to a million pounds to make, and that the BBC or ITV scheduler will rely on it to deliver an audience of 9 to 12 million contented viewers who will not only enjoy this episode, but turn on again the following week.

With so much at stake it is well worth commissioning three or even four scripts in order to get one that is good.

A 13-part series might therefore provide gainful employment to more than 25 writers. And still, at the end of the day, weak scripts will be accepted and go into production with the producers and script editor blindly relying on production values, in other words excitement on screen and glitzy casting – 'if in doubt cast up' – to save the day.

The writer shortage

The shortage of good writers in this area is acute. Script editors are often in despair, wondering where to turn next. All too often the choice is between the script editor's chum who works in the fringe theatre and rather despises television, or the weary old hack who has been churning them out since *Z Cars* and the first series of *Howard's Way*. When a new writer with sparkle, imagination and technical skill comes along he is sobbed over, cosseted, commissioned for new episodes and taken out for extravagant lunches. This could be you.

Step by step for the new writer

Select the series you would most like to write for.

1. In doing this, consider both your tastes in drama and any specialist knowledge you might have. A series about barristers will look favourably on a promising new writer who has been a barrister or a legal secretary; a series set in the medical world will always be interested in a script from a midwife or doctor.

2. Ideally, make your approach when the series is being transmitted and is getting a good audience response. This is often the time a decision on a further series is made.

3. Phone the production company that makes the programme and ask if a further series is planned.

4. Attempt to speak directly to the script editor or producer, and ask if they are willing to read an example of your work.

5. If they say 'yes' send them a copy of an original play you have written.

6. If you cannot speak directly to them, find out their names so that you can write to them personally.

7. Send an example of your writing. Say you would like the opportunity to submit a storyline. Ask if there will be changes to the basic format in the new series, i.e. are major characters being written-out, is the location changing? Ask for a copy of any new format notes for writers.

You can try to get new format notes during your first phone call, but the production office is unlikely to send out details of format changes to somebody who has phoned out of the blue and has not written for television before.

If the script editor is looking for new writers, though, and likes the writing sample you have sent, then she will encourage you to submit a storyline and will give you the same format notes that are being sent to experienced writers.

Common queries

Does it matter what sort of writing sample I send?
Yes. If you are hoping to write for *Heartbeat* it is not

helpful to send a gritty play about urban deprivation in Brixton. The script editor is trying to judge whether your talents for characterisation, dialogue and plotting would make you suitable for the series she is editing. Don't make life difficult for her.

Should I send an episode of the series I want to write for?
No. Editors are not impressed by pale imitations of what you are seeing on the screen, and you do not have the current information regarding format. Editors want an example of what you, the writer, do best on your own initiative: your own characters, dialogue and style.

Should I send in lots of ideas for the series to show my ability and interest?
Again you do not have the relevant format information, and editors are not really interested in storyline ideas until they know you have the ability to write. That said, if you put forward a first-class storyline, well structured and succinctly told, so gripping that the editor can't put it down – then you are likely to get an interested response.

How do I write a storyline?
You have to put forward, in a clear, easy to understand manner, the story you are proposing. You have to make it exciting to the reader. You have to show that your drama opens in an interesting way, sustains itself, and has a good ending. It does not matter if your storyline is one page or six pages long, if what you write does the job. But the following guidelines might be useful to the beginner.

- Give an interesting summary of your story or stories: 'Wealthy Sir Solomon Featherstone leaves £50,000 in his will so that his friends can enjoy the party of a lifetime. And so they do – until a group of shaken guests swear they saw Sir Solomon himself dancing at the disco. Det Insp Friday disinters the coffin – and uncovers more than he expects'.

- For a 50-minute series episode an editor will normally expect a three- or four-page storyline. (Between 500 and 1,200 words.)

- If you are writing for ITV the editor will look for strong endings to part one and part two – preferably edge-of-seat endings that keep viewers interested, and stop them from slipping away to other channels during the adverts.

- If the storyline has two or three strands – perhaps a main story, a secondary story and a comic sub-story – the editor will look to see how skilfully stories develop and intertwine, and how you propose to contrast quiet moments in one story with action in another (see Chapter 4).

- Take care not to get bogged down in detail – 'He says to her, then she goes out and he turns to somebody else and says...' – but stick to the main story developments. You are writing a synopsis not a blow-by-blow account.

SHORT PLAYS OR 'SHORTS'

Short plays – either 30-minute slots or the 10-minute slots pioneered by Anglia's *First Take* and *10x10* by BBC Bristol are usually aimed at encouraging new directors rather than new writers. It is the would-be director, often from film school, who approaches the television company with a show-reel of their work and a script. But where do the directors get their scripts from? They have little money to buy scripts, and no access to professional writers. If you have an idea for a film it is worth ringing film schools to see if there are talented unknown directors desperately seeking talented unknown writers. Check with the Film Council, which sponsors 'shorts' as part of its brief to 'develop and nurture emerging film making talent' and which operates not only in London but in Scotland, Wales, Northern Ireland, and the English regions (see chapter 18). Ring TAPS, a charitable organisation that runs excellent low-cost scriptwriting and comedy writing courses, holds competitions, and arranges rehearsed readings (see chapter 18). It is also worth ringing regional arts associations who bring together local writers and directors and occasionally help with co-funding. Watch Internet sites like the BBC's Writersroom (*www.bbc.co.uk/ writersroom*) and Channel 4 Ideas Factory (*www.ideas-factory.com*) for news of competitions or planned series.

Step by step for the new writer

◆ Watch any series of short dramas being broadcast and if you are confident that you could write for the slot (take into account the type of stories told, the number of characters, the mix of studio/video) note the name of the producer or script editor.

◆ Phone and ask if another series is planned. Ask if you can submit a script. Ask if the programme works in conjunction with any particular film schools or arts funding bodies.

- If you are directed to the BBC's Writersroom, send your script in with a covering letter saying the strand for which it is intended, and giving the name of the producer or script editor that you want to read it.

- Monitor Internet sites (like the Film Council regional and national sites, and writers' sites like Screenwriter Store, see chapter 18) that are likely to provide information about low-budget drama strands and/or competitions.

- Approach film schools and/or local arts associations to say that you are interested in writing a script for a new director.

- If you are in Scotland, Northern Ireland, or Wales, look at low-cost drama specific to where you live – like *Tartan Shorts* in Scotland.

- If the television production offices are non-committal, and the film schools not wildly enthusiastic, write a script anyway. This is only a ten-minute or 30-minute drama and you can afford to make the effort.

- Remember that 'shorts' are low budget – this means perhaps £15,000 to £50,000 – so the fewer actors you use the better. Also remember that 'shorts' are primarily aimed at developing director skills. Your story must have the potential to be visually interesting.

- Send your script to arts associations that encourage local writers, to film schools, to Channel 4's Independent Film and Video Department, and to the BBC's Writersroom. The BBC warns writers not to send uncommissioned and unrequested scripts to individual producers and programme production offices (saying that they always end up in the Writersroom anyway) but times change, and it does no harm to try your luck if you know a producer or script editor by name.

CHILDREN'S DRAMA

The requirement for children's drama is exactly the same as for any other kind of drama, be it one-off plays (of which very few are made) or series and serials (of which there are a lot). The BBC produces the most children's programming through Cbeebies aimed at 4–6 year olds, and CBBC focusing on 6–12 year olds. ITV has cut back drastically on its children's TV output, possibly because producers of sugary sweets are no longer allowed to advertise heavily within children's TV commercial breaks. Children's drama is almost always low budget (though *The Roman Mysteries* cost over £1m an hour to make) so historical dramas are more difficult to sell than contemporary themes. Classical adaptations often have period settings, but in this area experienced writers are always used. Prominent drama slots on CBBC are generally 15-minute dramas in the early evening aimed at 6–8 year olds, and 30-minute dramas, either original (like the comedy series *Young Dracula*) or adaptations at around 5pm.

Children's programming guidelines

When writing for children certain guidelines have to be observed which essentially means being careful with the following:

1. Situations arising from adoption, desertion, cruelty in the home, which could threaten a child's emotional security.

2. Portrayal of injury or disablement, or embarrassing personal disabilities like stuttering.

3. The use of weapons or poisons to cause injury or death.

4. Joke stunts that could be copied with disastrous results: stretching wire across a path, for example, to dismount a cyclist.

5. Heroes and heroines who smoke and drink alcohol.

6. The infliction of pain or humiliation on others. Suffering of children or animals.

BBC script guidelines

The BBC's Children's Development Unit warns against having very large casts, too many sets, exotic foreign locations, and massive special effects (although they add that a certain amount of 'magic' is fine.) They get too many scripts and ideas relating to pop bands, computer games, 'green' issues and time-slip stories. They advise new writers to bear the following in mind:

◆ Series or serials normally run for six episodes. Write the first episode and provide synopses of the rest.

◆ Do not have long speeches. Keep dialogue short and crisp.

◆ Make sure there is plenty of action.

◆ Keep the plot going, with constant new developments.

◆ Write short scenes.

◆ Start with something exciting that will grab attention.

SITUATION COMEDIES

Everybody is looking for comedy scriptwriters. They are the best paid writers, they are the most in demand – and they suffer the most rejection. Every year the BBC, ITV and Channel 4 produce their crop of new situation comedies (often from new writers) and every year the critics and viewers are mercilessly dismissive. For every *Vicar of Dibley* there are a clutch of sitcoms that bite the dust, desperately unfunny, mourned only by the sad writer who worked so hard at the jokes and the poor actors who had to play them.

Does the script run for 30 minutes (the standard narrative comedy length)? Does the script tell a self-contained story that introduces the main characters and sets up the series premise? Is the script consistently funny? Is every character three-dimensional, with a defined personality and recognisable tone of voice?

(BBC Comedy Department advice to new writers)

It is because comedy is so difficult to judge that both the BBC and ITV are prepared to spend large sums of money making pilot programmes of sitcoms, and why there are now several comedy workshops where scripts – often by new writers – can be tried out on live audiences.

What programme makers say they want

◆ Comedies that are 'intelligent, character-based, and up-market'.

- Stories that are unpredictable with twists to keep an audience guessing.

- Comedies which 'draw their strength from realistic and relevant situations and characters'. (BBC 1)

- Comedies that have a 'simple and funny high-concept premise which immediately suggests comic possibilities'. (BBC Comedy Script Unit)

- Comedies that will attract a younger audience and appeal to younger women. (BBC 2)

In all cases, these ideas must have the potential to generate and support future storylines.

What programme makers say they don't want

- Familiar themes: flat-sharing, the chap who's won the pools, mothers-in-law situation, grandads who come to stay and won't go home.

- Contrived situations and elaborate contrivances to keep the characters together.

> Take your characters up a tree and then lob rocks at them.
> (Caryn Mandabach, producer *Third Rock from the Sun*)

- 'Down-market, class-ridden comedies'. (ITV)

- Comedies that rely on 'strings of gags and funny lines'. (BBC) in other words the old time, third-rate ITV sitcom with artificial situations and farcical stories.

- Comedies that need expensive filming. Almost all situation comedy is studio-based, sometimes with a small amount of OB.

Step by step for the new writer

1. Use the Internet to find out about situation comedy competitions and current script development plans. The BBC site is *www.bbc.co.uk/newtalent/* and there is useful information on *www.bbc.co.uk/writersroom.* Look also at the BBC's Get Writing site (*www.bbc.co.uk/dna/getwriting)* and at Channel 4 Ideas Factory (*www.ideasfactory.tv*).

2. Write a brief outline of your idea, its premise, and your main characters. First try to sum up the idea in around 25 words (e.g. A sleepy, old-fashioned rural community suddenly finds its new vicar is a bubbly, enthusiastic, female who is determined to make things happen!). Your entire proposal should not be more than two pages long (well presented without too much dense writing) because the script reader will have already assessed several other proposals before reaching yours, and she will need all the mental assistance you can give her.

3. Write the first three half-hour episodes. Try to decide, as objectively as you can, which is the best (the best opening, the fastest, funniest story, and the really cracking ending). This is the script that you must send in. If it turns out to be the second or third script, ask yourself if it can possibly work as script one. If it can't, send it in with a brief outline of the series opening.

4. Send your script and outline to independent production companies as well as to the BBC. If an independent likes your idea they can offer it to the BBC, ITV, Channel 4, and Channel 5.

5. Send your script to independent producers who are making comedies that are currently being shown. They will be actively looking for new projects to replace programmes that are reaching the end of their life. (Situation comedies like *Fawlty Towers*, *Black Books*, and *The Office* burn brightly, but often only run for two or three short series).

6. If your script is rejected by the BBC don't let independent production companies know. 'My script has been turned down by the BBC but I thought you might still like to see it' might be honest, but it will not help you.

7. The BBC comedy unit likes scripts to be bound with a metal paper binder in the top left hand corner (which is how finished scripts are bound), and pleads for a self-addressed stamped envelope to be included.

8. See chapter 19 for addresses of programme makers.

9. Send your script and outline to at least two independent companies at the same time. If you go round the independents one by one you could be a hundred and receive your telegram from the Queen before you get the final rejection letter. If one company takes you up, you can tell the others that your work is no longer available.

10. Don't give up on a script too soon. Comedy is so individual that your work could be rejected by half a dozen producers – and then be taken up with

enthusiasm by the next. At the same time, if several producers give a very clear and consistent reason for rejection ('Dear Sitcom Writer, you may not have noticed but there has already been a comedy series about a jolly lady vicar in a rural community...') then they are probably telling you something that you ought to know.

14

Soap Operas

A LARGE AND GROWING MARKET

Many new writers get their first chance in television by writing for soap operas. Many stay in the world of 'soaps' and become seriously well-off, particularly those writing for the major serials – *Coronation Street*, *Eastenders*, and *Emmerdale*. Soap operas do not always succeed – *Families* and *Eldorado* were costly mistakes, ITV's relaunched *Crossroads* failed, as did the more critically approved *Night and Day*, but *Hollyoaks* has established itself, as has the BBC's *Doctors* with its slightly different format. ITV is once again actively seeking a new daytime soap, and such is the perceived public interest in soap operas that *Moving Wallpaper*, the comedy about a soap on ITV1, even had its mock-soap showing on ITV 2.

Some soap operas bring in extra money from overseas sales. *Jupiter Moon* can be seen on cable and satellite in the USA, and the Scottish Television soap *Take the High Road* was, for some reason, so popular in Sri Lanka that at one time it filled the Saturday evening prime-time slot.

Soap operas represent a huge market. Even the established soaps are using more writers, as they expand to make more programmes. At any given moment half-a-dozen script editors will be actively on the look-out for new writing talent.

<u>STORY SO FAR</u>

Pot-bellied, whisky-pickled union shop convenor BILL HODDER is all set for tomorrow's freebie visit to a Bayonne engineering works.

In the meantime he and wife LIZ have been promised a wedding-anniversary outing by son CLIVE.

CLIVE, though, has forgotten his filial duties and fixed a date with SANDRA BREWSTER.

JOHN SCHOFIELD, project engineer at Alfred Holt, is worried by a sudden, mystifying cut in development funds.

GILLIAN BREWSTER, 13, is within an ace of getting her own pony.

SANDRA BREWSTER is having a terrible time. Last week she was told she wasn't good enough for the shorthand/typing job her father FRANK got for her.

At the end of the last episode her father found out.

We last saw her sitting, anguished, on her bed, while FRANK stormed up the stairs....

Fig. 21. A serial drama script editor will write either a 'Story So Far' or an episode synopsis to accompany each script.

<u>1. INT. HALLWAY. BREWSTERS. DAY   (From Episode 11)</u>

Opening theme music as we see FRANK turn at the bottom of
the stairs and start to climb them, a grim, set look on his
face.

> FRANK
> Sandra! Sandra!

<u>2. INT. SANDRA'S BEDROOM.   DAY (From Episode 11)</u>

17 year-old SANDRA sits hunched up on her bed. Hearing her
father's voice she looks in distress towards the door.
She's for it now!

CUT TO:

OPENING TITLES

<u>3. SANDRA'S BEDROOM. DAY</u>

FADE IN on FRANK pacing up and down, exercising his powers
of mental creativity. SANDRA still sits hunched up on the
bed, but is now snivelling over a shorthand pad.

> FRANK
> And in conclusion I would like to express
> my gratitude for the esteemed honour---
>
> SANDRA
> We haven't done esteemed!
>
> FRANK
> The esteemed honour of the valued custom
> you have so kindly given to us---
>
> SANDRA
> I've never had esteemed said to me in me
> life---
>
> FRANK
> So kindly given to us and I confirm
> delivery of same by the fourteenth ult.

Fig. 22. A writer picks up the story from a previous episode – in this case there is a
reprise of the final scene of the previous programme.

To write for a soap opera you need to:

♦ take a lively interest in the domestic drama of everyday life

♦ respect popular drama and regard it as worthwhile and important

♦ have the ability to work with other writers, and to help formulate stories in storyline meetings

♦ be able to write imaginative, lively scripts within the restrictions of length, sets, locations and cast that are imposed

♦ thoroughly understand the nature of long-running serial drama: the 'soap formula'.

THE SOAP FORMULA

I remember, in those early days, likening the *Crossroads* cast to birds in a nest, with their beaks wide open, yelling for 'More plot, more dialogue, more problems, more solutions...'

(Reg Watson, producer of *Crossroads* and *Neighbours*)

Soap operas use up a ferocious amount of dramatic material. There are always at least three running stories that are not interconnected, and once those stories are exhausted new ones involving different characters must take their place.

The vital part of the formula is that we must be able to go, effortlessly, into the homes of our characters for an inexhaustible supply of domestic dramas.

There might be a big story of love and passion at Domicile A, a running tale of ambition and money at Domicile B and a running comedy theme at Domicile C. It is important that these dramas need only relate to each other (be it in the pub, shop, factory) when we want them to.

The simpler the structure and more ordinary the location the better. The identity of a soap opera is created by its characterisation, plotting and view of life, not by any originality or novelty in format.

SOAP OPERA STORIES

Soap operas are popular dramas, aimed at every age and class. They have inherited the mantle of the minstrel and the teller of folk tales, the mantle worn by Trollope and Dickens and a host of less talented but equally prolific writers. At their worst (and there is a lot of their worst) they are bland and repetitious; at their best they are as good as any drama on television.

Our audience is looking to see an immediacy and relevance to their lives, and this is particularly true among young people, for whom drama is one of their viewing preferences.

(BBC Drama Department)

Opinion polls have told us what viewers look for.

◆ Different generations of people – babies and teenagers, adults and senior citizens.

◆ Love affairs, engagements, marriages, divorces, and all the complications resulting from male-female relationships.

◆ Young people and young people's problems – teenage 'going off the rails', school activities.

◆ Young couples living together. Homebuilding, pregnancy, unemployment.

◆ Humour.

◆ Community gossip, scandal, intrigue and curiosity.

◆ Larger-than-life characters – rogues, tarts, stirrers, snobs, gossips... people that ordinary folk can identify with.

SCRIPTS AND WRITERS

If you have twelve writers on your team, then at any given moment at least two of them will be on the way out. A writer might be going abroad for a few months, or want to take time off to write a novel, or might simply want to get off the soap opera treadmill. Then again the writer might not know he is on the way out, that sadly his time will be up just as soon as the script editor can find a replacement.

Many writers are kept on the team long after the producer, editor and cast have been sent screaming mad by boring, empty dialogue, pathetic characterisation, repetitive and unimaginative scenes. They are kept on – often to their own surprise – because at the end of the day they can be relied on to deliver a script that:

- is the right length with a commercial break reasonably near the middle

- has the right number of characters

- uses the right sets with the right amount of OB

- covers the stories that the storyline says it should cover

- does not steal stories the storyline has allocated to the next writer.

The script editor opens the tired writer's script with a sinking heart, knowing she is going to have to stay up half the night trying to inject a modicum of sparkle and believability into the dialogue – but also knowing that on a primitive, basic level the script will work. It won't have to be binned. It will be pretty awful, but the cast will act their little socks off and it will get by.

And in the meantime, the search for a replacement writer will continue.

Step by step for the new writer

The first thing you must do is to choose your soap opera.

1. Identify the soap opera that you, as a viewer, most enjoy watching.

Among the urban TV soaps *Coronation Street* and *Eastenders* are identical in structure (working-class homes focusing on a pub; one in its time had a factory making jeans and the other a street market selling them), but vastly different in style. *Coronation Street* draws strength from Northern values and Northern humour, and often gives us a laugh. *Eastenders* reflects, indeed, sometimes seems to prey on, a glum world where life is gritty and grim. *Emmerdale* has its own characteristics, and they are far from being the characteristics of *Hollyoaks*. There was once a writer who, using two names, was on the team of both *Coronation Street* and *Crossroads*, but generally speaking writers are faithful to one programme because their view of life and writing style suits only one programme.

2.   Identify the programme you are best qualified to write for.

It might seem that if you grew up on a farm in Yorkshire, trained as a vet, regard all southerners as effete, and would rather go down a coal mine than watch dramas about lesbians, then you would find a warm welcome on *Emmerdale*. In fact, you would be better off – assuming you can write brilliant dialogue and have a good sense of humour – at *Coronation Street*.

3. Have a sample of work to show.

Evidence of your ability is vital. Editors want to see how you handle characters, plots and above all dialogue. In the first instance editors usually prefer to see a single play you have written and do not want to see your attempt at writing their soap opera.

Make sure your writing sample is something that will help the script editor to assess your suitability – in other words contemporary drama based on dialogue and character rather than action.

4. Find out the name of the script editor, either by watching the credits or by phoning the production office.

5. If you do phone the production office ask if the programme has its own system of assessing new writers – trial scripts, perhaps, or new writers' seminars.

6. Send your sample script with a short covering letter.

If there is something in your background you think might be useful (you've been a social worker/vet; you're the Director of Programmes's mistress/boyfriend), say so. Otherwise the letter should be short and to the point, as in the example shown in Figure 23 on page 175.

7. Make sure you know the programme thoroughly.

If the script editor likes your original script she will either write encouraging you to submit a trial sample script (unpaid!), or she will speak to you on the phone (curious to know more about you) or invite you in to talk.

If you are lucky she will just have had one writer bundled into a drying-out clinic, another run off to Latin America, and been forced by the producer to sack another. If you are unlucky the programme will have recently received three or four scripts from very promising new writers, and not be looking for more.

Either way, you have to be ready. You have to know about the programme – the characters, the locations, the stories in recent episodes. You must be able to say, instantly, what the current three running stories are. You must be able to say which characters you think are being written well for, and which are not. You must be able to project enthusiasm and have sensible, realistic ideas.

If you are encouraged to write a sample script, ask for a couple of back scripts, preferably by different writers, and any writers' guidance notes that exist.

8. Do not copy the style of other writers.

Other writers' scripts, and episodes you have taped and studied, will give you a feel for the programme. But the script editor is not looking for a pale imitation of the past, she is looking for dialogue that is new and fresh; characters that ring true and honest, but are illuminated in a brighter, more vivid, more believable way; stories that are developed with verve and energy.

What next?
Assume your sample script was brilliant and you have been commissioned to write an episode. The script editor will not object to being sent flowers at this point. You will be asked to the studio, shown round the set, lunched in the canteen. You are a professional writer. Congratulations! You now have your first **scriptmeeting** to face.

How soap operas are written
Every soap opera varies slightly in its script production methods. Some programmes (like *Eastenders*) try to give scriptwriters an element of creative freedom, other soaps

Ms Zia Wanascript
'Coronenders'
Friendly Television Company,
Moneygalore Road
London 1AA 6BQ

9 June 200X

Dear Zia Wanascript

I am interested in writing for Coronenders and enclose as
an example of my work a 60-minute television play called
'Promise'.

I would be happy to write a sample script for Coronenders if
you think this would be worthwhile.

If so, I would be grateful for any guidance notes for writers
that you might have.

(or)

I understand that you occasionally hold seminars for new
writers. I would be grateful for the chance to attend one of
these.

I hope you enjoy reading 'Promise'.

Your sincerely

Julian Goodwriter

Fig. 23. How to write a covering letter for a sample script.

are very much a production line, with every scene, and the reaction of every character to every event, mapped out by storyliners. What follows is a typical fortnight on one of the more chaotic soaps.

> I like to write with the world shut out and completely naked. Who knows -- some of the stuff I write might not be as good if I had kept my kit on.
> (Al Hunter Ashton, *Eastenders* script writer)

Scriptmeeting

Up to a dozen writers meet for a day with the producer, two script editors and storyliners. They already have a long-term storyline. On this occasion they thrash out the stories for a fortnight of episodes. At this point the writers do not know which episode they will write or even if they will write at all. They are expected to contribute ideas for all the episodes. If they do not show keenness and enthusiasm, they might not be commissioned to write.

Scripts commissioned

The storyliners (who are almost always young, stressed-out, would-be writers themselves) work feverishly to prepare a storyline for each episode, showing commercial breaks and episode cliffhangers. Writers are phoned and offered an episode. They are told the schedule this time is very tight, and that they can only have four days to write their script.

Storyline approved

There is a delay while producers and executive producers read the storylines and demand changes. Writers are phoned and told that their storylines are going to be late, but will be faxed or e-mailed to them. They ask if they can have a later delivery time. They are told no they can't.

Episodes written

The storylines reach the writers. They start work. After several hours they are phoned again and told that their storyline has to be changed because of story objections from the channel head of drama. Writers again ask if they can have a later delivery date. Again they are told no they can't.

Scripts back

The scripts come in, often by e-mail, and are edited by the script editors. Rewrites might be demanded by phone or fax, and will need to be completed within a matter of hours. The scripts go to the producer, then to the script typist, and then into production.

The storyliners are already preparing for the next scriptmeeting...

Six weeks or so later

The episodes are made, both in the studio and on location. On five-episodes-a-week soaps there is little or no rehearsal.

15

Other Markets for Scripts

Almost all television work for freelance writers is in drama and situation comedy, but a few opportunities exist in other areas.

CHILDREN'S PROGRAMMES

Children's drama has been covered in Chapter 13. Otherwise opportunities are few. The BBC uses some unpublished stories and says that ideas for children's programmes will be considered. Writers, it is said, should watch the department's output carefully to see the types of programmes being made.

For ITV watch the output carefully, note which regional company (or Independent) is putting Children's ITV on the network, and then approach the executive producer directly.

EDUCATION

The BBC transmits more than 2,000 hours of educational programming each year, an amount roughly matched by ITV and Channel 4. Many schools programmes are drama or dramatised documentary and ought, in theory, to provide excellent opportunities for new writers. The BBC says, however, that most of its schools programmes are written either by the producer or by a teacher/academic who has been approached by the production team.

Apart from schools broadcasting, BBC Education is looking for history programmes that encourage an active interest by viewers, for programmes that deal with citizenship and the community, and for programmes that deal with parenting. Costs must be similar to daytime prices (see below).

For ITV and Channel 4 note the television companies making the programme in which you are interested, and ring them directly (for contacts see Chapter 19).

SCIENCE PROGRAMMES

Most writers are expected to be involved with the actual production – which in practice means that writers are either BBC staff, or experts approached by either the production team or the independent production company that has been commissioned to make the programme. The BBC stresses, however, that consideration is given to scripts or ideas that are sent in. It is clearly an advantage to be an expert – if your idea is a programme showing the bizarre effects of quantum mechanics on daily life it is more likely to be taken seriously if you are a physicist rather than a stockbroker.

Treatments should be about two or three pages long, outlining the subject and making clear the way the writer would tackle the script.

HISTORY PROGRAMMES

The BBC and Channel 4 have discovered the appeal of history in recent years, and although most resources go into series like *Timeteam* and *Meet the Ancestors* there is a market for one-off features and part series, and these often include scripted sequences, even if it is only cavemen sitting round a fire going 'Ug'. If you have an idea for a history programme featuring dramatised sequences your best option is to approach an independent company that has a track record making historical documentaries. If they think the idea has appeal, they can put the proposal forward as a package.

LIGHT ENTERTAINMENT

Comedy sketch shows use a huge amount of material and there is a market for freelance sketches and one-liners. The BBC is at pains to say 'that there is no call for comic songs or verse'. Write directly to the producer of the show you are interested in, or to the head of light entertainment at ITV and Channel 4 and the BBC.

HUMAN INTEREST, CONSUMERS AND LEISURE

This is a vast and growing area of television. There are innumerable programmes about cookery and gardening, and specific interest programmes like *Sky at Night* and *Crimewatch UK*. Sadly there is virtually no work here for the freelance writer, but ideas and formats are always wanted. What next after the fashion for house-buying programmes pioneered by *Location, Location, Location* and *Property Ladder*? What next after the success of 'makeover' programmes pioneered by Trinny and Susannah? Many commissioning editors and daytime TV controllers would like to know the answer.

See which independent production companies are making the programmes you like, and approach them directly with your own idea.

DAYTIME TELEVISION

Daytime television is invariably low cost. In practice this means that the BBC expects to pay an independent company around £15,000 for a 30-minute programme. There is a market for documentary series (like *City Hospital*), panel games, quizzes, and interactive topical shows (i.e. chat shows). If you can come up with an idea for a 25–40 minute documentary type programme that only costs £4,000 then BBC 2 would love to hear from you (programmes in this area normally utilize news or sports archive material). Again, your best bet is to make an approach through an independent.

SCOTTISH, WELSH, IRISH AND REGIONAL PROGRAMMING

Both the BBC and ITV in Scotland, Wales and Ulster devote resources to programmes that will not be shown throughout the United Kingdom and which reflect Scottish, Welsh and Irish interests. BBC Scotland, for example, is the BBC's most varied production centre outside London. Apart from making the short film drama series *Tartan Shorts* and the Scottish soap *River City* it makes factual programmes like *End of Story* and *Writing Scotland* – both designed to encourage writing talent. BBC Wales not only produces the soap opera *Pobol y Cwm* but also drama-documentaries specifically for Wales.

Watch output, identify the slots devoted to regional programming, and if you have an idea approach the producer.

All the main ITV companies make programmes for their own regions. The BBC makes specific regional programmes from Birmingham, Newcastle, Manchester, Bristol and Plymouth. Again, watch the regional slots (usually on BBC 2) and if you have an idea, write to the producer.

Telephone numbers for BBC and ITV production centres are included in Chapter 19.

We aim to add more peak time talent to our schedule. We should also be a launch pad for bright, new talent both on-screen.and off – a place of enterprise and creativity.

(Jane Lush, Head of BBC Daytime Commissioning)

16

Common Queries

CHARACTER LISTS

Should I include a list of characters at the front of the script?

Yes, but keep it short, don't worry about minor characters and make your descriptions pithy and pertinent. 'Julian is late forties, a chartered accountant, married for around 20 years to Rose. The only apparent interest in their lives is who will reach the menopause first.' Do not write half a page of description on each character, and do not insist that they be tall or short or red-haired or bald, unless this characteristic is vital to the story.

SYNOPSES

Should I include a synopsis of the story?

A short indication of what the play is about – perhaps 50 or 100 word – can be useful in that it tells the script editor the sort of play she is about to read. 'A man claiming to be an MI6 agent breaks into a remote Welsh farmhouse. He tells the farmer and his family that he is pursuing a cell of cult fanatics intent on poisoning the water in a nearby reservoir. But why won't he say who he plans to meet at the farmhouse? And why does he force the family, at gunpoint, to hand over their mobile phones?'

This gives the editor a good idea of what is to come – a drama about a family torn out of normality into a nightmare situation. Even better, ITV's 2007 two-part thriller *Instinct* was summarised in production as 'a talented young detective's traumatic past returns to haunt him during the hunt for a serial killer stalking the Lancashire Pennines.' This is the kind of synopsis that will engage a script editor's interest. She will go on reading to see how well or badly you tackle the subject.

Do not write a three- or four-page synopsis. The script editor or professional reader might just as well read the play, and anyway the reader will be required to write a synopsis to prove that she has read the script carefully.

PROTECTING YOUR WRITTEN COPYRIGHT

Do I need to write 'copyright' and put a 'C' inside a circle?

It is curious but true that the very worst writers submitting the most unlikely scripts are those most anxious not to have their material stolen – and they very often put on their script a very firm copyright line. Very few professional writers or agents do this (your work is your copyright whether you draw little circles on it or not), although it is always a good idea to put the date on each draft you submit. If you want to protect your script further you can register it with the **Writers' Guild** providing you

Ideas don't interest us in themselves... Ultimately there is no point in stealing ideas, since ideas are never in short supply. What is rare is the writer who can take a good idea and execute it well.

(BBC Writersroom)

are a member (see page 229), or you can seal a copy in an envelope and send it to yourself by registered mail, and then keep the package unopened. There are also enterprising Internet sites (e.g. *www.thescriptvault.com*) that will register and store your script electronically for you.

PROTECTING YOUR IDEAS

Will my ideas be stolen?

If they are going to be stolen, a copyright line will not help you. Many unsuccessful writers are convinced that their ideas have been stolen and used later, and it is easy to see how suspicions are aroused. A writer sends in an outline for a series of dramas set in a university, say, and it is rejected. Then, a year later, a university series pops up on the *same channel* that rejected his idea!

There have always been university/student ideas floating around, just as there have always been outlines for series set in airports, hospitals, city parks, animal sanctuaries, riding stables, factories.... There have recently been two rival proposals for series set on trains.

It must have happened that a writer's work has been stolen but it is a very unlikely occurrence. Nobody is going to plagiarise an actual script – they have no need to. If your script is good they will buy it anyway, and besides you would be very likely to find out and complain. Again if your idea for a series is *very specific* nobody is going to be foolish enough to try to pass it off as their own.

There is, however, a grey area when it comes to ideas. Say you have submitted an idea for a comedy series about two rival pleasure boat operators on the Thames. The idea is read and rejected. A year later the editor who rejected you is involved in another project, and suddenly has a flash of brilliance: 'We could have a chap who hires rowing boats, and somebody could try to move in on his patch...'

The editor has probably no idea where the thought came from. Even if she does remember your offering she will not regard the idea as exclusively yours. Intellectual copyright is a very difficult area of law, but basically you cannot copyright ideas (unless they are worked out in detail) and you cannot copyright titles.

SCRIPTING COMMERCIAL BREAKS

Are there rules about where to put the commercial break?

Officially, yes, but they are sometimes ignored. The established IBA rule is that the scene following a commercial break must be either (a) in a different location to the scene immediately before the commercial break, or (b) there must have been a time lapse of at least five minutes in your drama.

In other words you cannot do this:

DIANE: OK, right, so who is
the little tart?

MARTIN: This is not doing any
good, this is just upsetting you.

DIANE: Will you tell me who
she is, damn you!

MARTIN LOOKS UP, SUDDENLY DEFIANT

MARTIN: OK, if you really want
to know.

COMMERCIAL BREAK

SCENE FIVE. THE KITCHEN AS IN SCENE
FOUR

MARTIN: The woman I am leaving you for is Lisa Strombali from the petfood factory.

DIANE: My best friend Lisa?
You rat!

The scene before the commercial break is fine. After the
break you would need to assume a short time lapse and
preferably take us to a different location.

SCENE FIVE. EXT. PARK. DAY. DIANE IS
LEANING OVER THE FOOTBRIDGE. MARTIN
IS WITH HER.

DIANE: I suppose you met her
at the petfood factory.

MARTIN: Yes.

And so on.

Must the commercial break be exactly halfway through the script?

It is more important that it should come at a natural, dramatically effective point.

That said, a 30-minute slot on ITV is just over 24 minutes long, and it is usual for the break to be somewhere in the middle four minutes.

A one-hour serial or series slot is 52 minutes long, and generally has two commercial breaks. The first should be at least 15 minutes into the script, and the last not less than 15 minutes from the end.

When submitting to the BBC *take the breaks out.*

HOW TO TIME SCRIPTS

How do I time my script?

If you follow either of the script layouts suggested in Figures 1 and 2 on pages 113 and 114 your script will be running at around 45 seconds a page – depending, of course, on the pace and mood of the play and the amount of description you include.

If you read your script out aloud (preferably with another person, alternating lines), and also *read out loud the movements of the characters and action sequences*, you will get a rough timing. Nobody expects more of you at this stage.

SCRIPT LAYOUT

Why do television scripts only use the right-hand side of the page?

There are three versions of a television script.

1. The first is by the writer, and is written for the script editor and producer to read. There is no practical reason why this should only run down half the page – it is wasteful and leads to high postage costs. However, it is commonly done.

2. The second version is the rehearsal script, typed up by the production secretary after the first version has been edited, rewritten, changed for continuity, or cut for time. This version traditionally runs down the right-hand side of the page so that:

3. The director's PA can add the camera directions to the production secretary's computer file without having to retype it. And in the studio or on location, the PA and floor managers can use the left-hand space to make continuity notes.

The examples in Figures 24, 25 and 26 on pages 190–192 are from a studio play, and show these three versions of the script.

What if my script is altered?

For a script editor to alter your script and rewrite bits presupposes that you are in the happy position of having sold it, that your script is in production and other creative influences are now at work.

<u>3. CAFE</u>
DAISY brings ANNA a coffee and sits with her.

             DAISY
             Did you go to the meeting? Did he ask you out?

             ANNA
             Yes I went and no he didn't. I don't know why -
             I can't understand it. I wore my best suit, you
             know, the pretend Chanel one with the little
             gold chains.

             DAISY
             To a <u>CND</u> meeting?

             ANNA
             There's no reason not to look my best, Daisy,
             whatever the occasion. And my black patent
             heels, because Simon's so tall I thought he
             wouldn't feel threatened.

             DAISY

             No. Well what happened?

             ANNA
             What happened? They kept talking about the bomb
             and all that sort of thing, that's what
             happened.

             DAISY
             They would at a CND meeting. I don't think you
             take it seriously.

ANNA chokes on her coffee.

             ANNA
             Seriously - my God I'm dead serious! I joined
             didn't I? If Simon doesn't ask me out soon I
             don't know what else I can do-·

Fig. 24. A page as originally written.

```
                    SCENE 5    THE CAFE

---------------------------------------------------------------


                         DAISY
                         ANNA

                  DAISY
                  All I meant was he might notice you
                  more if you could talk to him about
                  his interests.

                  ANNA
                  I've joined CND.  I went on a march
                  - in my red slingbacks with four
                  inch heels all through London, past
                  all the shops and I didn't go in,
                  not even down Sloane Street.   I can
                  talk about his interests. I don't
                  suppose he's going to want me to
                  know more about them than he does.

                  DAISY
                  No ---

                  ANNA
                  Men never do.  He gave me a lift
                  home after the meeting.

                  DAISY
                  You see!  He must like you.

                  ANNA
                  He must, really, mustn't he.  Well,
                  I did ask him if he would.  I left
                  my car at home on purpose and said I
                  had a tube phobia.



            - 13 -
```

Fig. 25. The rehearsal script.

DAISY COMES OVER WITH HER PAD.

DAISY
One egg mayonaise and salad, three
coffees and a chocolate fudge cake.

See DAISY in +
hold her away L to
2S DAISY/GIORGIO

GIORGIO
We need more egg mayo, OK?

DAISY GOES THROUGH TO THE KITCHEN.

52. 3   GIORGIO
     CU GIORGIO   I saw a traffic warden
                  earlier. I hope your cab's all
53. 5   right out there. /
     CU A?B

                  BRIAN
54. 2   She won't bother my cab. What were
     2S GIORGIO/MARIA   we saying about Gustavus Adolphus. /

     /5 repo KitchenL/
                  MARIA
                  (PATIENTLY) Gustavus Adolphus, the
Hold 2S with her Swedish Meteor, took Pomerania in
cross   1630 only to face the obstacle of
                  Brandenburg and Saxony.

                  GIORGIO
Hold her away R to (WHISPERS) Stop encouraging him.
BRIAN & ease in to CU
                  BRIAN
                  That's right. Now then, a lot of
                  people have got the wrong end of the
                  stick about the 30 years war.

/SHOT 55 ON 5 NEXT/   END OF SCENE

Fig. 26. The camera script.

Essentially, having accepted several thousand pounds for a script, it is no longer your property: at least not insofar as the rights you have sold are concerned. After all, if you buy a chair and take it home you can do what you like with it – chop a bit off one leg because of your uneven floor, or add a structural support – and you do not expect the carpenter to come and interfere and shout at you.

I regard myself as a storyteller, a narrative playwright, so a successful series episode, to me, is one in which I have managed to write my own original play within the framework of the series, without anyone noticing.

(N.J. Crisp, writer)

In practice, having bought the script the television company can cut it, but cannot *add lines* without informing you, the writer. You cannot actually stop them adding lines – but if you disagree strongly, you can take your name off the play.

IMPORTANCE OF TITLES

How important are titles?
It is quite likely that the script editor will first open and start to read your script without even looking at the title. Many television plays – and in particular series – go through half a dozen titles (known as **working titles**) before the final name is agreed.

There is no doubt that a strong title is a good thing, and titles with sexual connotations and hints of intrigue always do well: *Desperate Housewives, Bad Girls, Footballers' Wives, Mistresses, The Year of the Sex Olympics.* Action titles are good: *Licking Hitler* and *Spend, Spend, Spend* and titles that conjure up memorable images like *The Saliva Milkshake* and *Deadhead.* There is a theory in America that any title with a number in it cannot fail: *The Third Man, The Fourth Protocol, Beverley Hills 90210* – and indeed it is said that films are now being made with titles like *Godmother 6* without there having been any Godmothers one to five.

ARE AGENTS NECESSARY?

Do I need an agent?

A good agent is an enormous help. A good agent is known and respected by producers. When a script from such an agent arrives on a producer's desk it is taken seriously, read quickly, and the assumption right from the start is that it is good. Many programmes (like *The Bill*) say they will not look at a script at all unless it comes through an agent.

It is unlikely, as a new writer, that an agent can get you a higher fee than you could get for yourself. But an agent will make sure your residual rights and repeat fees are as they ought to be particularly when dealing with independent production companies.

The problem is: how do you get a good agent to take you on? Good agents are careful to guard their reputation. They will not send a script to a producer unless they have confidence in it. They will not take on a writer unless they are confident in his ability. Persuading a decent agent to read your script and take you up is probably as difficult as getting a television company to buy your script in the first place.

If you approach a top television agent you are likely to be told that she already has more writers than she can handle, and is not looking for new clients at the moment. Occasionally this might be true. But at the end of the day all agents are interested in new, exciting writers – it is the ten per cent of your talent that keeps them fat and prosperous and if you have genuine ability an agent will eventually take you up and devote much time and effort to helping you.

It is best to approach an agent once you have either:

◆ won a playwriting competition, particularly one for television, or a London pub theatre writing competition, or

◆ had at least one play – either for television or radio – accepted.

A list of agents dealing in TV scripts is on page 244.

HOW MUCH YOU WILL BE PAID

How much will I be paid?

Writing for television is generally considered lucrative – but some slots pay a lot more than others, often because they attract automatic repeat fees. A good agent will fight to get you as much as possible, but most series and serials pay set rates, particularly for new writers. If you don't have an agent you can check on current agreements with the Writers' Guild or – a wise move – you can join the Society of Authors and they will check through your contract for you free of charge (see Chapter 18, page 228).

Some examples of television drama fees:

♦ A new writer will get around £12,000 for a 90-minute original television play. This might sound a lot, but is actually not much for many weeks – if not months, or years – of work. If the programmes is reshown or 'bought out' the writer will get a further payment – often 100%.

♦ On the other hand, an established writer will be paid up to £6,000 for an episode of a 30-minute soap opera like *Hollyoaks* that has been largely storylined by others, and that will take less than a week to write.

♦ A 45-minute script in a BBC series like *Robin Hood* will pay an experienced writer around £15,000 (plus fees for other rights).

♦ An ITV series like *Heartbeat* or BBC series like *Holby City* will earn more than £6,000 for a new writer, and around £10,000 for an established writer.

♦ *The Bill* pays a new writer around £12,000 and an experienced writer over £17,000 – and there can be further fees from foreign sales.

♦ An episode of *Eastenders* will earn around £8,500 including the omnibus fee.

- Writers become 'established' after writing four or five scripts. A good agent will make sure it happens sooner rather than later.

- BBC and ITV rates of payment are now very similar (ITV used to pay much more).

- Channel 5 pays less.

- Independent Production companies have been notorious for asking writers to work on ideas, storylines, and scripts, without payment. Producers that belong to the Independent Producers' Association, PACT, will pay writers to develop a storyline (between 5% and 10% of an eventual script fee) or a treatment (between 15% and 25% of an eventual script fee). In practice, though, a new writer will still be expected to do a great deal of work without payment in order to show that they can deliver what they promise.

- The rate for children's drama or educational drama series and serials (both areas where the new writer might find an opening) is around £90 a minute, though in practice much higher rates can be paid on prestige projects. Religious drama, if there were ever to be any, would be paid at the same rate.

- When you are invited to attend the read-through of your script and attend rehearsals, you will be paid around £85 a day, and the BBC and ITV faithfully promise to pay this within 30 days of attendance.

- The most lucrative work is on serials or series where one writer writes all the episodes. A three part original serial, with each episode running for 90 minutes, will earn the writer around £75,000 – and the possibility of at least as much again from overseas sales and repeats.

♦ An established writer on a soap opera like *Coronation Street* who also has income from previous programmes (residuals) might easily earn in excess of £150,000 a year.

♦ If you are a poet, however, and one of your published poems is read on television, you will be paid around £30 per half minute, and might well starve to death.

17

TV Talk: Common Words and Expressions Used in Scripts and in the Television Industry

Action props
Props used by actors in the course of a scene – swords if there is a sword fight, pen and paper if the scene calls for them to be used. The food consumed on set is an action prop.

Ambient noise
Background noise like traffic or air-conditioning. Often referred to as 'atmos'.

Backing
In the studio a piece of scenery put behind a door so that we do not see the studio when characters go in and out. Windows on sets similarly have backing scenery.

BCU
Big close up. The camera shows only part of the face or object.

Bible
When a drama series is given the go-ahead the first thing to be commissioned from the creator is the Bible. This is a full format with story idea, setting, locations, notes on style,

character notes and usually the initial storylines.

Binned

A script is 'binned' if it is not acceptable and cannot be re-written. The writer will already have been paid 50 per cent of the fee, but will not be entitled to the 'second half fee' if the script is not accepted. In practice writers are often paid the full amount in order to shut them up.

Boom

The microphone is held over the actors' heads on a boom or poked towards them behind the furniture. If you see actors on location, strolling over the hills with not a boom in sight, it means that either the sound operator is disguised as a sheep or the actors are using radio microphones.

Camera script

A studio script with the camera moves and technical directions on it. (See Figure 26, page 192.)

Captions

Opening captions show the title of the play or series, the individual episode title if there is one, the creator, the leading actors and usually the writer.

Ciné-vérite

Fly-on-the-wall documentary style, often involving a hand-held camera, giving a feeling of realism.

Credits

The names of actors, production staff and crew, and usually the producer and director. It used to be the case that the director always had the final credit, on a caption all to himself, but television is increasingly a producers' medium, and producers (or executive producers) are commonly taking the last place. To achieve this without aggravation directors are now sometimes credited among the opening captions. They like this because it is what happens on feature films.

CU

Close up. The face of a character or object fills the screen.

Cut away

If you want to leave a scene or set for a moment, to indicate a time lapse perhaps, or remind us of things happening elsewhere, or to give pace to a scene, the quick shot of something else is called a cut away. For instance, a tense scene of a couple waiting for a blackmailer to turn up might be interspaced with cut aways to show the blackmailer in his car driving towards the house, parking, coming up to the door. Or a scene showing a character dashing to save a victim might include quick cut aways of the victim bound and gagged and suffering terrible things.

Day for night

Filming on location at night is extremely expensive. Every shot has to be separately lit, which involves unbelievable numbers of electricians, exorbitant hire charges on lighting equipment, and massive overtime payments to the crew (this last item is changing as independent companies negotiate more effectively than the old ITV companies).

A traditional way to include night scenes on a low budget is to shoot during the day but with special filters on the camera. This day for night trick results in sequences that look murky and have strange colour tones. However skilled the cameraman, the sky is usually much too bright. Directors and producers dislike having to shoot day for night.

DBS

Direct satellite broadcasting.

Digibeta

Broadcast quality digital videotape, a format commonly used for shooting drama.

Digital editing

It used to be that when you copied tape it lost quality – 'went down a generation' – but digital technology means that edits can be dissolved and then reformed as new. Practically all editing – sound and picture – is now done digitally. Editors can do marvellous things, but cynics note that editing tape now takes ten times as long and costs ten times as much as it did in the old days when you had a piece of film and a razor blade.

Dress

A set is dressed when it has all its bits and pieces in place – cushions, tablecloth, ornaments, the movable items that have been stored away to stop them being stolen or damaged while the set was not being used.

Dry

An actor dries when he totally forgets his lines.

Dubbing mixer

Or sound supervisor. The person who mixes and adjusts sound effects, dialogue and music once the programme is filmed or recorded.

Ext or Int

Exterior or interior.
Although still very commonly used, Int and Ext survive from the days when Int meant anything done in the studio, and Ext was the bit of exterior shooting to show characters out and about in the world.

Nowadays most dramas are shot entirely on location, either on film or video, and directions as to Int or

Ext are often superfluous. The direction INT. JULIA'S BATH-ROOM is pointless, unless there is a possibility that Julia's bathroom might be open to the skies, or somebody might be clinging to the outside wall peering in. The description EXT. EXMOOR is equally redundant, as INT. EXMOOR would be a nonsense. Int and Ext are still used, however.

Extras

Actors who do not have lines and are not individually and specifically directed to carry out particular actions. People sitting drinking and chatting in the background of the Rover's Return are extras. Generally speaking writers need not worry about extras – the production will hire as many or few as it can afford. It is not a good idea, however, to write a play that positively must have a battalion of the Grenadier Guards milling around – you are likely to end up with four or five extras desperately trying to look like a battalion by moving about a lot.

Extras who are required to speak or to actually do something are called **walk ons**. A walk on can have ten words or so and can be directed.

Thus if the barmaid in the Rover's Return says 'Now then Charlie, what was it a pint of mild?' and an extra nods and says, 'That's right' the extra will be classified as a walk on and be paid a few pounds more. Similarly if you want us to come across your hero entwined in the arms of a beautiful girl who is kissing him passionately and murmuring 'Cuddlebundle', the actress will be a walk on providing she does not say 'cuddlebundle' more than ten times and providing it is agreed that 'cuddlebundle' is one word and not two. The eleventh 'cuddlebundle' will officially, though not in practice, qualify her as a speaking character and put up her fee from around £100 to around £400. In practice actors are grateful for every word given because it increases their exposure on television.

Lines for a walk on should not be written in the script as dialogue but given to the actor on the day. You should thus write:

9. INT. DISCO. NIGHT

WE DISCOVER RORY IN CLOSE EMBRACE WITH YET ANOTHER BLONDE. SHE IS MURMURING WORDS OF ENDEARMENT AS MARIAN APPROACHES AND STARES AT THEM WITH A GRIM EXPRESSION.

Fade to black　　When you want the screen to go to black, often used between scenes as a time passage. This device used to be popular, then was regarded as terribly clumsy, and now is regarded by some as quite artistic. American dramas tend to fade to black every few minutes, but this is because the advertising breaks have been taken out.

Film editor　　The film editor or VT (videotape) editor assembles the programme from the material shot, usually under the instruction of the director. In film the first assembly or **rough cut** will be viewed by the producer and script editor, who make their comments. A writer should endeavour to be present at this stage, although there may be resistance.

Fluff　　When an actor muddles up a line or says the wrong word. An actor who does this will often do it again and again, at exactly the same place. Sometimes this is because of stress and tension – studio time costs hundreds of pounds every minute – and sometimes because the line or word is genuinely difficult to say. 'Probably' is often a word to cause fluffs, and actors will always thank you for writing 'I expect I'll potter to Pettifers' rather than 'I'll probably potter to Pettifers'.

Footprint   Satellites have different 'footprints' – their programmer can only be seen on television sets within their area of broadcasting as they travel round the Earth.

Format   A document explaining an idea for a series or soap opera. A format is usually about ten pages long. A shorter document of two or three pages might be called an **outline.** Nobody knows which term is correct and nobody really cares. (See also **Bible**.)

Genre   A type of programme. Soap opera is a genre. So is science fiction. Critics, script editors, director and producers are all fond of the word.

Gun mike   A microphone that operates in a very narrow band, but over a long distance. It can be used to pick up the speech of an individual in a crowd.

High angle shot/ low angle shot
The camera looking down or looking up.

Indie
Independent production companies are known as Indies. Twenty-five per cent of television production is supposed to be made by Indies. Some of them are very big like Working Title and Pearson, but others are very small – often just one or two hopeful people working from home with a phone, fax, and headed notepaper saying Megaworld Productions UK Ltd.

In frame
A person or object is in the camera's view.

In the can
A scene that is 'in the can' has been successfully (technically, if not artistically) recorded or filmed.

Libel
When your script is commissioned you will sign a contract stating that you will use your best endeavours to ensure that no defamatory matter is included in your work. The most obvious danger of libel comes from the choice of a character's name, or the name of a place. On page 23 there is an outline for a play about a

man called Slime who starves to death the residents of the Hardtimes Residential Home for the Elderly. If this play were transmitted and it transpired that there really was a Mr Slime in charge of a Hardtimes Residential Home for the Elderly then he would be likely to claim damages for defamation of character.

The trouble with a real television play is that you cannot fall back on patently invented names like Slime.

So what can you do to protect yourself?

Basically, you should be certain that you have *not* libelled somebody you know. If there is an accountant called Fidgetwig living next to you, do not write a play about a crooked wife-beating animal-loathing accountant called Fodgetwog, because your neighbour will successfully sue you and the television company for a large amount of money.

In practice the script editor will carry out what is called a **neg check**. Thus if you have a crooked security organisation in your play a check will be made (there are specialist firms who do this) on company registers to make sure that no security organisation with the name you have chosen actually exists.

Using a very common name is not necessarily a protection. It is true that if you call a sex maniac teacher Smith, you will not be liable for prosecution by the thousands of teachers called Smith in Britain. But if your play is about a sex maniac teacher Smith who has four daughters, a water spaniel and a Volvo and lives in Chipping Dodsbury, and after transmission you get a call from a Mr Smith of Chipping Dodsbury who has four daughters, a King Charles Spaniel and a Saab – then you are in big trouble.

Again, though, the television company will in practice have done a neg check on teachers in the Chipping Dodsbury locality.

Library film Film or videotape material not shot specifically for your play. If you have a scene with a teacher explaining the life cycle of the kangaroo, you might ask to see library film of kangaroos on a video screen behind the teacher's head. Use of library film is costed at so much per second, and the price depends on whether the production needs UK rights or world rights. Don't write it in without consulting the script editor.

LS

Long shot – figures in distance, obviously not possible in a studio production.

Mix

Cross fade as it is known in radio, or **dissolve** on film, is when one scene merges gently into the next rather than a straight **cut**.

MLS

Medium long shot – generally a group of figures.

MS

Mid shot – this would show figures from about the waist up.

Narrative

The narrative is the story told through the plot. It is what happens scene by scene, and when script editors says a script has a strong narrative they mean that on the superficial storytelling level it holds their attention and develops well.

A script can have a strong narrative and still be empty of new ideas or originality.

OB

Filmed, or recorded on video, away from the studio.

Off the page	Good dialogue is said to come 'off the page' if it has energy and life and is believable. It is very bad news when a script editor says: 'This dialogue just doesn't come off the page'.
Option	If a television company or independent production company wants to adapt a novel they first take out an option with the copyright owner, usually the writer. Even small independent production companies take out options, as this then gives them a 'property' that nobody else can touch during the period of the option. (See page 149.)
Offline edit	Working on videotape rather than film, the director uses a small offline edit suite to produce the equivalent of a film rough cut or first assembly. This saves time when the director moves into the vastly more expensive **online edit suite** where the final editing actually takes place.
OOV	Out of vision. Sometimes called **OS** (**off screen**). We are listening to a character who is in the scene but is not visible. (But see VO below.)
Pan	The camera remains in a static position but the lens moves along a

	row of people, round a room, or across a landscape. The camera does not change its focus.
POV	The camera shows us something from a particular character's point of view.
Producer's run	When studio plays (nowadays mainly soap operas) have been rehearsed and actors are 'off the book' (know their lines) the play is run through without costumes or cameras for the producer and script editor to watch. At this point the producer can cut things and change interpretations she does not like, and the script editor can insist that the actors go back to the lines that were written for them, rather than the ones they've made up in rehearsal.
Production values	Are what everybody wants. If a show has good production values it means that visually the budget is being well spent, that the show looks lavish and interesting without costing an arm and a leg.
Pull back	The camera pulls back from a close up or medium shot to show more of the scene.
Reader	Most ITV companies and large

independent production companies employ readers to assess unsolicited scripts. These readers are often would-be script editors, usually female, often not long out of university. They are paid anything between £20 and £75 to read your script. They then have to summarise the story (to prove they have read it through) and give their opinion in around 100 words. Readers are sometimes more skilled and perceptive than you might expect.

Read through

On the first day of production the cast, technical staff, production staff and the writer come together for the first time, to read through the play. Whilst some actors are happy to give a performance, others read through the lines in a dull monotone. This is not because they dislike the play, but because they dislike interpreting the lines before rehearsal.

Residuals

The extra money you get when your play is repeated in the UK or sold elsewhere in the world. (See **How much will I be paid?**, page 195.)

Script unit

The BBC has a script unit that processes 10,000 unsolicited scripts a year and the bigger ITV companies and Indies have heads of drama development (often young graduates from Oxford who want to work in television). Readers are employed to process unsolicited material (see Chapter 19). Often they will give useful advice if they think you show ability. Unlike script editors assigned to particular programmes who are paid to find an exact number of scripts to fill an exact number of slots and do not have time or inclination to run a free advice service, script editors working with script units have a duty to encourage and help promising talent.

The drawback is that however much a script unit editor likes your work she is never in a position actually to *buy it*. At the end of the day it is a producer or editor working on a series hat you have to please.

SFX   Sound effects. Denotes a particular sound effect that you want over a shot – if somebody is lying in bed dreaming about the sea and you want the sound of seagulls it would be an SFX. Rather old-fashioned radio phrase – it is as easy to write 'we hear the sound of seagulls and crashing waves'.

Slow zoom　　The camera moves slowly in.

Stock shot　　A shot that can be used over and over again. Often a three- or four-second shot of the exterior of a house in a series or serial drama.

Storyline　　In series drama, a storyline is what the writer submits. It gives the basic story and shows the development of the plot stage by stage. In soap operas the storyline is drawn up by the script editors and details the stories that will be covered by individual writers. (See page 126).

Talking heads　　A play in which people talk to each other all the time, in boring locations, without any action. 'Talking heads' is generally regarded as a pejorative expression. 'It's nothing but talking heads' a director will moan.

Tighten　　A zoom in, but gently and not as dramatic or as much.

Tracking shot　　The camera moves with the characters – perhaps two people walking towards us, and the camera moving away at the same speed. The camera itself can also track in on a group. This is different from the **zoom** in that the camera itself moves, so that the angle on the subjects changes. We might, for example, start on the backs of the two characters as they sit on a sofa, and then track round with the camera until we see their faces.

Treatment

Development of an idea, showing how it will break down scene by scene, and often including examples of dialogue.

Two hander

A scene with only two characters.

Two shot (2S)

Two people on the screen.

VO

Voice over. A narrator voicing over a scene in a sound studio, or dialogue from scene A that is put over scene B for artistic effect.

Whip pan

A pan at speed – again not used in studio and only when being artistic on film.

Working title

If a writer cannot think up a good title for a play or series he gives it a working title just to be going on with. On the first page this will be indicated by:

BOOT MAN
(Working Title)
by Veronica Jane Rumble

Wrap   The time recording or filming ends.
                     A location will wrap at a certain
                     time. 'It's a wrap' means that
                     shooting has finished for the day.
                     'We wrapped at one minute to six,'
                     says the production manager to the
                     associate producer, who is worried
                     about overtime.

Zoom   The camera focus moves in or out on
                     a person or object.

18

Organisations That Will Help You

- Writing courses
- Residential courses, day seminars, and workshops
- Grants and development funds
- Internet help sites for new writers
- Writers' organisations
- University courses.

WRITING COURSES

Your aim, at all times, should be to *make contact with a professional, working, script editor.* Sending a script cold through the post might be your only option if you live in the Orkneys (where script editors rarely stray in a professional capacity) but for those able to do so, attending scriptwriting courses can prove fruitful. Some examples:

- A biochemist with no contacts in the television world attended a weekend writing seminar in the Cotswolds (advertised in *The Guardian*) and her script was assessed by a professional working script editor. She went on to write for *Eastenders*.

- Three young graduates on a scriptwriting course at the Northern Media School, Sheffield, were among students who had their work assessed by an assistant producer from Channel 5. They were all offered contracts on *Family Affairs*.

♦ A young playwright attended a TV-writing course organised at the Liverpool Playhouse. His script was read by a senior script editor from Thames TV. He went on to write for *The Bill*.

When you consider a scriptwriting course of any kind you should always look carefully at the quality of advice you will be getting.

♦ DO go for scriptwriting courses where your work will be looked at by professionals currently working in the industry. Always, if you can, opt for a course where you meet your tutor.

♦ BE WARY OF courses where the tutors are media-course academics who have never actually worked in television – or are said to have had a distinguished career in as script consultants on TV drama in the Seventies.

♦ BE VERY WARY of correspondence courses. Quality of advice can be very uneven. You might be given an able tutor who has recently worked in television, but you might equally get somebody who has never worked in the business at all. Always ask to be told your tutor's credits. Avoid courses which ask you to do 'exercises' or to keep revising a piece of work. Some of the correspondence writing schools that advertise 'your money back if you have not sold a script by the end of the course' are reputable and give sound advice – but, clearly, there are not many people who ever finish their courses. You are better off improving your skills by writing new 10-minute dramas that have a chance of being bought and made into programmes.

◆ Quality advice is not always cheap. A professional script editor or producer working on a major top-twenty series is not going to assess scripts by unknown authors for £5 an hour. Consultancies can charge up to £100 for a script analysis. Some residential week-ends cost over £400. On the other hand, professional working script editors sometimes attend seminars and short courses run by arts associations, universities, and organisations like TAPS and the Screenwriters' Work-shop (see below). These might be heavily subsidised or even free to local aspiring writers.

◆ Check with your local arts association on forthcoming scriptwriting courses (often run by university depart-ments of continuing education) and writers' organisa-tions in your area.

◆ Look out for scriptwriting courses advertised on Internet sites like Script Factory (*www.Scriptfactory. co.uk*) or in Scriptwriter Magazine (*www.scriptwriter magazine.com*). Avoid courses aimed primarily at feature film screenwriters, unless you enjoy delving into the theory of script structure and want to know how to write film treatments and make a 'pitch'.

RESIDENTIAL COURSES, DAY SEMINARS, AND WORKSHOPS

Residential writing courses, seminars, and workshops are usually run by enthusiasts and can be excellent – but they often survive for only a few years and then, sadly, fade away. As with everything else, check on the Internet to see what is on offer. Three organisations that are well-established and have a high reputation are the Screenwriters' Workshop, TAPS (Training and Performance Showcase), and the Arvon Foundation.

The Screenwriters' Workshop

Formerly the London Screenwriters' Workshop, it helps new writers with seminars, workshop events, and tuition. The largest organisation of its kind in Europe, the workshop was founded in 1983 by a group of film and television writers as a forum for contact, discussion, and practical criticism. Courses cover every aspect of script writing, from how to write a treatment to how to do a re-write. Some courses last for several weeks, other subjects are covered in afternoon or evening workshops. There is also a script reading service that offers a professional assessment of your script with suggestions on storylines, character, plot, and dialogue.

The Screenwriters' Workshop,
Suffolk House, 1-8 Whitfield Place,
London WIT 5JV.
Tel: 020 7387 5511
email: *screenoffice@tiscali.co.uk*
Website: *www.lsw.org.uk*

TAPS

TAPS (Training and Performance Showcase) runs workshops, courses, and competitions in various parts of the UK, and is very focussed on developing the creative and technical skills that will enable new scriptwriters to get their first commission. Promising writers are invited to workshops and given professional training. The best scripts are given rehearsed readings. People who have attended TAPS workshops are now working on series like *Eastenders, Coronation Street* and *The Bill.* If you go to a TAPS workshop, or course, you are likely to meet script editors and producers who are currently working in the business.

TAPS,
Shepperton Studios,
Shepperton,
Middlesex,
TW17 0QD
Tel: 01932 592151
email: *jill@tapsnet.org*
website: *www.tapsnet.org*

The Arvon Foundation

High quality guest tutors run five-day residential courses at Hebden Bridge in Yorkshire, Totleigh Barton in Devon, Craven Arms in Shropshire, and Beauly in Inverness-shire. The foundation runs courses in many forms of creative writing, including film scriptwriting, television comedy and television drama. Courses are informal and friendly – students and tutors make their own breakfasts and lunches and share the cooking of the evening meal – and are open to anybody over the age of 16. The foundation is supported by the English and Scottish Arts Councils. Fees are low – around £450 including accommodation and food – and there are various bursaries available.

The Arvon Foundation,
Totleigh Barton,
Sheepwash,
Devon EX21 5NS
Tel: 01409 231338
email: *t-barton@arvonfoundation.org*
Website: *www.arvonfoundation.org*

GRANTS AND DEVELOPMENT FUNDS

Arts Council
The Arts Council works through Arts Wales (*www.arts-wales.org.uk*) Scottish Arts (*www.scottisharts.org.uk*), and regional offices covering the East of England, the East Midlands, London, the North East, North West, South East, South West, West Midlands, and Yorkshire. Information is now very much Internet-based. Look at the main website and you will be directed to the different regional sites where you can find contact numbers to get information about pending writers' festivals, scriptwriting workshops, or drama events.
Tel: 0845 300 6200
Website*: www.artscouncil.org.uk*

Euroscript
A curious but admirable EU scheme to promote European scriptwriting. It provides funding to develop several screenplays a year, runs a film story competition (deadlines are 30 April and 31 October each year) and supports international workshops. In the UK it lives at the same address as the Screenwriters' Workshop (see above).

Tel: 020 7387 5880
email: *info@euroscript.co.uk*
Website: *www.euroscript.co.uk*

UK Film Council

The UK Film Council is primarily concerned with funding aspiring filmmakers – but this can often involve funding scripts, particularly for short films. Check its website for details of current script funding in the different regions – North East, North West, Yorkshire and the Humber, East of England, East Midlands, West Midlands, the South East, and the South West.

The Film Council
10 Little Portland Street
London W1W 7JG
Tel: 020 7861 7861
Website: (*www.ukfilmcouncil.org.uk/regions*)

Film London

Part of the Film Council, it gives grants to writers, producers, and directors in the capital. Send a sae for details or look at the website.

Film London
20 Euston Centre,
London NW1 3JH
020 7387 8787
website: *www.filmlondon.org.uk*

PAWS Drama Fund

PAWS (Public Awareness of Science) drama fund gives grants to writers (currently £2,000) who come up with good ideas for science-based television drama, and also organises informal discussion evenings where scientists outline areas of their work they believe have dramatic potential, and television drama producers add their comments. There is generally an opportunity for writers to talk informally to both the scientists and the television people (it's the television people you want to meet!). PAWS is supported by companies like Zeneca, BP, and Unilever. For details write to:

> PAWS,
> 1st Floor
> 155 Regent's Park Road
> London NW1 8BB
> 020 7483 4545
> email: *pawsomni@globalnet.co.uk*

INTERNET HELP SITES FOR NEW WRITERS

Three excellent sites for the new writer are:

BBC Writersroom (*www.bbc.co.uk/writersroom*) has onward-going details of BBC drama requirements, competitions, Internet-based scriptwriting help, and script assessment.

Scriptwriter Magazine (*www.scriptwritermagazine.com*) has a website that gives valuable information about scriptwriting seminars and provides links to other writers' sites. The magazine is published bi-monthly, and works closely with the Writers' Guild.

Writing for Performance (*www.writing.org.uk*) gives excellent free advice and valuable links to other sites. It is particularly strong on situation comedy.

Other sites worth looking at are:

BBC Get Writing (*www.bbc.co.uk/dna/getwriting*) encourages new writers to talk to each other and publish their own work on the Internet.

BBC Talent (*www.bbc.co.uk/talent*) is another BBC initiative to discover and promote new writers and performers. Look at this site for details of competitions and regional events.

Farnham Films (*www.farnfilm.com*) is one of the most useful sites on the net. It provide a list of TV drama commissioning editors – invaluable as the list is regularly updated – and has plenty of advice for new writers.

Ideas Factory (*www.ideasfactory.com*) works very closely with Channel 4 and provides online masterclasses covering topics like 'Writing dialogue' 'Developing character' and 'Story structure'.

Ideas4writers *(www.ideas4writers.co.uk)* is not specifically aimed at script writers, but provides useful links to other sites.

Screenwriters' Store (*www.screenwriterstore.co.uk*) sells software and training material, and provides news about courses and workshops for new writers.

Scriptfactory (*www.scriptfactory.co.uk*) – provides training and development for scriptwriters, and is sponsored by organisations that include the UK film Council, and BBC Films.

Scriptunities (*www.xerif.com*) lists all UK and European script competitions, and links to scriptwriting workshops at Birbeck College, University of London.

Write4Television *(www.write4television.co.uk)* offers online writing courses and professional script assessment.

The Script Vault (*www.thescriptvault.com*) will archive your script electronically (thus helping to protect your copyright), and offers a script assessment service.

Writernet (*www.writernet.co.uk*) is designed to provide a comprehensive service both for writers and producers and covers theatre, television, and film.

ORGANISATIONS FOR WRITERS

The Society of Authors has an active broadcasting section with more than 800 members. There are occasional talks given by people working in the television industry – often producers and editors. The society has a permanent staff, including a solicitor who will vet contracts for you (useful if you do not have an agent). The society will take legal action on your behalf if the issue is considered of general concern to the profession. The society's magazine *The Author* comes out four times a year and has a broadcasting section which sometimes gives information about scripts in demand. The society also publishes free guides on such subjects as television agreements, copyright, libel, and authors' agents. If you do not qualify for membership of the society (you need to have had work accepted for publication or broadcast) you can buy *The Author* on subscription. There is also a category of associate membership for those who have not yet had a full-length work broadcast but have either received a major contract or have had occasional items broadcast. More information can be obtained from:

The Society of Authors
84 Drayton Gardens
London SW10 9SB
Tel: 020 7373 6642
Website: *www.societyofauthors.net*

The Writers' Guild of Great Britain negotiates television fees (and radio fees jointly with the *Society of Authors*) and gives help and advice on everything from contracts and agents to fees. The Guild holds frequent meetings for members, and publishes a very useful range of booklets. If you are not a professional writer, the Guild has a category of membership specifically for those 'who are taking their first steps in writing but who have not as yet received a contract'. For information on membership, contact:

The Writers' Guild
15 Britannia Street,
London WC1X 9JN
Tel: 020 7833 0777
Website: *www.writersguild.org.uk*

UNIVERSITY COURSES

Astonishingly, more than fifty universities or colleges in the United Kingdom currently offer MA courses in creative writing or scriptwriting. Before embarking on what might seem an arduous, and expensive, way to learn the writer's craft, ask if the course will include lectures, seminars, and (most particularly) script assessment by producers or script editors currently working in the industry. If there is no contact with the actual world of televison drama, the course is unlikely to help you to become a professional scriptwriter.

Universities offering courses that focus on film and television scriptwriting include:

Liverpool John Moores University
St James Road,
Liverpool LI 7BR
Tel: 0151 231 5052

University of Salford
Adelphi, Peru Street,
Salford M3 6EQ
Tel: 0161 295 6027

University of Sheffield
388 Glossop Road,
Sheffield S10 2JA
Tel: 0114 222 8177

Leicester De Montfort University
The Gateway,
Leicester LE1 9BH
Tel: 0116 255 1551

University of Glamorgan
Treforest,
Pontypridd,
CF37 1DL
Tel: 01443 482570

King's College,
University of London,
Strand,
London WC2R 2LS
Tel: 020 7848 2184

University of York
Heslington,
York YO10 5DD
Tel: 01904 433369

National Film and Television School,
Station Road,
Beaconsfield,
Bucks HP9 1LG
Tel: 01494 671234

19

Where to Send Your Script

APPROACHING A SCRIPT EDITOR

♦ You now have to get a producer or script editor to read your calling card script.

♦ Send a copy of your script to the BBC Writersroom. If you want to write for a particular programme (e.g *Eastenders*) say so. If your script shows promise it will be forwarded to the producer or script editor concerned. Alternatively you might be invited to meet a BBC script editor, or to take part in a workshop.

♦ As well as sending your script to the Writersroom, it does no harm to send a script directly to an editor or producer if you believe it will appeal to them. (The BBC discourages this approach and the producer concerned will probably pass it unread to the Writers-room, but you never know...)

♦ With ITV and the Independents, try to find out the name of the script editor or script executive – either from the on-screen credits, by a telephone call to the programme company switchboard, or by looking at the company's website.

♦ If you are a bold person, phone them and in a confident voice ask to speak to the script editor by name. Nine times out of ten you will not be put through, but you might be lucky. If you are, tell them you know they've got plenty of writers, but you would be grateful for any advice – do they perhaps have a writers' pack that they could send you? Try to engage their sympathy without irritating them. Ask if they will look at a script as an example of your work.

♦ Whether you have made contact or not, send your script directly to the person you want to read it. If you've spoken to them on the phone, make your letter personal ('Thank you for your advice. As discussed on the phone, here's my script *Happy Days*. It was good of you to offer to read it.') Keep your letter short but friendly.

♦ A good excuse for a phone call is to check on any special seasons for new writing talent, or to ask if the company produces a writers' pack for a particular programme.

♦ Send a copy of your script to the BBC Writersroom and to at least one other possible buyer.

Things you should NOT do:

♦ DON'T send a tatty manuscript decorated with coffee ring stains.

♦ DON'T tell the script reader things about yourself that are not relevant, eg: the funny incident at Ibiza that first made you become interested in writing; the friends who said 'You've got a real gift for words'.

♦ DON'T mention that your script has been turned down by others, eg: 'Morag Veryweary at ITV

Yorkshire read *Happy Days* with interest but unfortunately was not producing plays of this type at the moment and regretfully had to return it to me. Nat Goaway at Granada also liked it very much but felt he had to return it as he would not have a slot until Autumn 2049...'

Main drama department addresses are listed below, as are the names of some drama department contacts. People move about rapidly in the television world. Before sending in your script, telephone to make sure that the office holders have not changed (a good website for this is *www.farnfilm.com*).

BBC CONTACT ADDRESSES

BBC Writersroom
First Floor, Grafton House, 371–389 Euston Road, London NW1 3AU. This is the home of the BBC's 'new writing initiative'. The BBC promises that all scripts sent in (some 10,000 a year) will be read and considered for the initiative's 'highly targeted writing schemes and workshops'.

◆ Don't send scripts via email.

◆ Don't send ideas or treatments, or novels/short stories you might like to adapt.

◆ Don't send scripts for existing programmes (like *Eastenders*).

◆ Chase up you script if you have not had a response in three months.

Drama
BBC Television Centre, Wood Lane, London W12 7SB.
Tel: 020 8743 8000.

Controller, Drama Commissioning: Jane Tranter
Controller, Continuing Drama Series: John Yorke
Head of Development, Continuing Drama Series: Belinda Campbell
Head of Drama Series and Serials: Laura Mackie

Children's Drama (CBBC)
CBBC used to look at unsolicited scripts, but now wants new writers to make an approach via the Writersroom. If you feel like chancing your luck, you could pretend to be an established writer and make an approach directly via Development Executive Amanda Gabbitas or Head of CBBC Drama John East at:

CBBC Drama Submissions, Room E1200, East Tower, BBC Television Centre, Wood Lane, London W12 7RJ.
Tel: 020 8743 8000.

Comedy
BBC Television Centre, Wood Lane, London W12 7RJ.
Tel: 020 8743 8000.

Head of Comedy Commissioning: Lucy Lumsden
Head of Comedy: Jon Plowman

Learning and Interactive
BBC White City, 201 Wood Lane, London W12 7TS.
Tel: 020 8752 5252.

Controller: Liz Cleaver

This new unit commissions online and interactive factual programmes rather than drama – but it is looking for new writers.

Northern Ireland

Broadcasting House, Belfast BT2 8HQ.
Tel: 028 9033 8000
website: *www.bbc.co.uk/ni*

Produces a wide range of drama programmes including serials and single dramas. Will look at unsolicited scripts.

Development: Susan Carson
Head of Drama: Patrick Spence

Scotland

Broadcasting House, Queen Margaret Drive, Glasgow G12 8DG.
Tel: 0141 339 8844
Website: *www.bbc.co.uk/scotland*

The most varied production centre outside London. Watch its website for opportunities for new Scottish writers.

Head of Drama: Anne Mensah
Commissioning Editor, television: Ewan Angus

Wales

Broadcasting House, Llandaff, Cardiff CF5 2YQ.

Tel: 029 2032 2000.
Website: *www.bbc.co.uk/wales*

Broadcasts the Welsh soap opera *Pobol y Cwm* and produces popular drama documentaries and education programmes for network transmission.

Head of Drama: Julie Gardner

INDEPENDENT TELEVISION

Channel 4 Television
124 Horseferry Road, London SW1P 2TX.
Tel: 020 396 4444.
Website: *www. channel4.com*

Head of drama: Tessa Ross
Editor, series: Camilla Campbell
Editor, events: Ben Stoll
Senior commissioning editor, drama: Francis Hopkinson
Commissioning editor, drama: Lisa Marshall
Assistant editor, drama: Liz Philling

Channel 4 commissions programmes from independent companies and buys in ready-made programmes, but does not make programmes itself. Channel 4's remit is to provide programmes of interest to minority audiences and to be distinct and different from other channels. It aims at the 16 to 34 age group. Channel 4 says it is developing long running series alongside big event dramas. 'Any series should be based around a bold, provocative idea'.

Channel 5

22 Long Acre, London WC2E 9LY.
Tel: 020 7550 5555
Website: *www.five.co.uk*

Is committed to spend the money saved from *Family Affairs* on popular drama. Watch the website and send in ideas and scripts (always low budget).

Drama editor: Abigail Webber
Director of Programmes: Kevin Lygo

ITV Network Ltd

website: *www.itv.co.uk*

Controller, Drama: Nick Elliot
Head of Drama Series: Corinne Hollingworth

Broadcasts on ITV1 and ITV2. Check the website to see the drama series and serials coming up, and which production companies are making them. The ITV companies that make up the network do not encourage unsolicited scripts, but the big companies (now pretty well amalgamated within Granada) do make a lot of drama.

ITV Granada/ITV Productions

Granada Television Centre, Quay Street, Manchester M60 9EA.
Tel: 0161 832 7211.

Upper Ground, London SE1 9LT.
Tel: 020 7620 1620.

Website: *granadatv.co.uk*

Head of drama: Hugh Warren
Head of drama, Manchester: Kieran Roberts
Controller of drama, Manchester: Carolyn Reynolds
Controller of drama, ITV Productions London: Michele Buck
Head of Factual drama: Jeff Pope
Director of Children's drama: John Whiston

ITV Wales

ITV Wales, The Television Centre, Culverhouse Cross, Cardiff CF5 6XJ.
Tel: 029 2059 0590.
Website *www.itvwales.com*

Head of drama (ITV Wales): Peter Edwards
Head of development, indie productions: Sue Shephard

Scottish Television (STV)

Pacific Quay, Glasgow GS1 1PQ
Tel: 0141 300 3000
Website: *www.stv.tv/*

Controller of Drama: Eric Coulter

Makes drama and children's programmes for the ITV network, including *Taggart* and *McCallum*. Ideas for long-running series and serials are said to be welcome (with or without a Scottish flavour).

ITV Yorkshire

The Television Centre, Leeds LS3 1JS.
Tel: 0113 243 8283.
Website: *www.itv.com*

Group controller of drama: Keith Richardson
Controller drama features and comedy: David Reynolds

If you are interested in writing for *Emmerdale* note down
the name of the current producer or story editor from the
screen and send your calling card script (not your attempt
at an *Emmerdale* script) to them directly.

BSkyB

Grant Way, Isleworth, Middlesex TW7 5QD.
Tel: 020 7705 3000.
Website: *www.sky.com*

Drama commissioning Sky 1: Elaine Pyke
Head of film: William Turner

Now making a profit, there are hopes that BskyB will
plough money back into drama commissioned from
independents.

INDEPENDENT PRODUCTION COMPANIES

Some independents are bigger and more important than
many of the smaller ITV companies. Other independents
are one-person affairs that occupy West End offices when
they're in production, and shrink back into the spare
bedroom in Hendon when they're back 'in development'.
Big or small, however, there is little enthusiasm for

reading unsolicited scripts and offering constructive advice to new writers.

WARNING: Beware of independent production companies that want you to develop your work without a fee. A company might well say: 'Get this script right and we'll bust a gut trying to get it on...' Busting a gut in this context means that you spend weeks revising your script and the independent producer takes a Channel 4 commissioning editor to lunch and rapidly pitches a dozen different projects – including yours – in the hope that *one* will go forward into development. Too many writers are hacking away for nothing, paid only with words of encouragement and visions of hope. A company that really believes in your script will put money on the table, even if it is only a storyline or treatment fee.

Most independent production companies live in a state of flux. They come and go, amalgamate, change their names, change their address; and their willingness to read scripts changes just as abruptly, depending on their need for new ideas and their current staff levels. An Indie can have a Head of Script Development one week and just a part-time cleaning lady the next. Few, at any time, will admit that they welcome unsolicited scripts – but at the end of the day, of course, they can't do without new writers, scripts, storylines, and ideas. It's best to ring up, first, to find out what (if anything) they are looking for. Below are some of the Indies that make television drama and comedy.

The Comedy Unit

Glasgow TV and Film Studios, The Media Park, Craigmont St, Glasgow G20 9BT.
Tel: 0141 305 666.

Contact: Niall Clark, script editor.

Develops scripted comedy series particularly for children's television. Encourages new writers, and asks for material to be submitted by post or by email (*comedyunit @comedyunit.co.uk*).

Convergence Productions

10–14 Crown Street, London W3 8SB.
Tel: 020 8993 3666.

Contact: Helen Stroud, Head of development.

Noel Gay Television

Shepperton Studios, Studios Road, Shepperton TW17 0QD.
Tel: 01932 592569.

Asks for 1–2 page treatments. Contact: Charles Armitage

Hat Trick Productions

10 Livonia Street, London W1F 8AF.
Tel: 020 7434 2451.

Contact: Jimmy Mulville

Specialises in situation comedy and drama comedy. Check the website: *www.Hatrick.com*

Hartswood Films Ltd

Twickenham Studies, St Margarets, London TW1 2AW.
Tel: 020 8607 8736

Drama and comedy. Contact: Elaine Cameron

September Films

Glen House, 22 Glenthorne Road, London W6 0NG.
Tel: 020 8563 9393.
Website: *www.septemberfilms.com*

Contact: Elaine Day

Factual and documentary specialist now looking to expand further into TV drama and film.

Talkback Thames Productions

20–21 Newman Street, London WIT 1PG.
Tel: 020 7861 8000.

Send your script to: PA to Managing Director.

Specialises, very successfully, in situation comedy and popular drama, including *Green Wing* and *The Bill*.

Tiger Aspect Productions

5 Soho Square, London WIV 5DE.
Tel: 020 7434 6700.

Check the website: *www.tigeraspect.co.uk*

Wall to Wall Television

8–9 Spring Place, London NW5 3ER.

Tel: 020 7267 5292.

Working Title
76 Oxford Street, London W1D IBS.
Tel: 020 7307 3000 (films) and
77 Shaftesbury Avenue, London W1V 8HQ.
Tel: 020 7494 4001 (television).
Website: *www.workingtitlefilms.com*

Head of development, films: Debra Hayward
Head of television: Simon Wright

Says no unsolicited scripts at present, but you can always give them a ring and offer a treatment or outline.

Zenith Entertainment Ltd
43–45 Dorset Street, London W1U 7NA.
Tel: 020 7224 2440.

email: general@zenith-entertainment.co.uk

Head of drama: Adrian Bate

Television drama and serials, from *Hamish Macbeth* to *Two Thousand Acres of Sky*.

Doesn't encourage unsolicited scripts. Try an outline.

TELEVISION AGENTS
As with independent production companies, agents are private businesses that cannot afford to spend time reading and commenting on scripts that they do not

believe – if only from a cursory look at the subject matter and first page of dialogue – are going to make it. At the same time, of course, agents need new writers. You are always, therefore, in with a chance.

◆ Look in *The Writer's Handbook* or the *Writers' and Artists' Year Book* for agents willing to look at scripts or outlines by new writers.

◆ Give a succinct account of yourself, your ambitions and your circumstances. The agent will want to be assured that you have the determination, as well as talent, to be a full-time professional writer if the opportunity arises.

◆ Indicate the type of programmes you believe you could write for.

◆ Make sure your script is laid out in a clear and professional manner.

◆ ALWAYS enclose a stamped, addressed envelope.

Below are some agents who specialise in television work, are interested in new writers, and in some cases are willing to look at unsolicited scripts.

The Agency (London) Ltd.
24 Pottery Lane, London W11 4LZ.
Tel: 020 7727 1346.
Email: *info@theagency.co.uk*

Founded in 1995, The Agency brings together a number of London's most distinguished television agents. You will need to have won a scriptwriting award or competition, or had a script on radio or the stage, to be considered. Send a preliminary letter describing yourself and outlining your script.

Blake Friedmann Ltd.
122 Arlington Road, London NW1 7HP.
Tel: 020 7284 0408.

Contact for scripts: Julian Friedman.

Send letter with a synopsis and sample pages.

Casarotto Ramsay Ltd.
National House, 60–66 Wardour Street, London W1V 2ND.
Tel: 020 7287 4450.
Email: *agents@casarotto.uk.com*.

Send a preliminary letter describing yourself and outlining your script.

Curtis Brown Ltd.
Haymarket House, 28–29 Haymarket, London SW1Y 4SP.
Tel: 020 7396 0110.
Email: *cb@curtisbrown.co.uk*

Contact: Nick Marston

One of the biggest and most respected agencies, handling television scripts of all kinds. Send a preliminary letter describing yourself and outlining your script.

Jill Foster
9 Barb Mews, Brook Green, London W6 7PA.
Tel: 020 7602 1263.

Particularly interested in TV comedy and drama. Send a preliminary letter describing yourself and outlining your script.

David Higham Associates
5–8 Lower John Street, London W1R 4HA.
Tel: 020 7434 5900.
Email: *dha@davidhigham.co.uk.*

Send preliminary letter with synopsis in first instance.

Valerie Hoskins Associates.
20 Charlotte Street, London W1T 2NA.
Tel: 020 7637 4493.
Email: *vha@vhassociates.co.uk*

Contact: Valerie Hoskins or Rebecca Watson.

Specialises in film, television and radio. Send a preliminary letter describing yourself and outlining your script.

Andrew Mann Ltd
1 Old Compton Street, London W1D 5JA.
Tel: 020 7734 4751.

Email: *Manuscript@onetel.com*

Contact: Anne Drew, Tina Betts, Sacha Elliot.

Send a preliminary letter, synopsis, and sample pages of script. Email your letter and synopsis if you wish, but attachments will not be opened.

PDF

Drury House, 34–43 Russell Street, London WC2B 5HA.
Tel: 020 7344 1000.
Email: *postmaster@pfd.co.uk*
Website: *www.pdf.co.uk*

Peter Fraser and Dunlop, as it used to be known, is one of the most respected and successful agencies in the world – and what is more, it will look at scripts by unknown writers (perhaps this is why it has become so successful). Look at the website for script submission guidelines, or send your script to the 'Film and Script Dept' making sure you enclose return postage.

Sheil Land Associates.

43 Doughty Street, London WC1N 2LH.
Tel: 020 7405 9351.
Email: *info@sheilland.co.uk*

This agency 'welcomes approaches from new clients either to start or to develop their careers.' Send a preliminary letter first, describing yourself and outlining your script.

Further Reading

TV PLAYS

Some are paperbacks currently in print, others can be ordered through libraries.

Plays that might be said to have influenced contemporary television drama are marked:*.

Soldier, Soldier, John Arden (Methuen, 1967). *Soldier, Soldier* was broadcast in 1960; one of the first great television plays by one of Britain's most important playwrights.

*Talking Heads**, Alan Bennett (BBC Books, 1988); The *Writer in Disguise* (Faber and Faber, 1985).

*The Boys from the Blackstuff**, Alan Bleasdale (Granada, 1983); *The Monocled Mutineer**, (Hutchinson, 1986).

*The After Dinner Game**, Malcolm Bradbury (with Christopher Bigsby) (Arrow Books, 1989). Four plays for television.

*Deadhead**, Howard Brenton (Methuen, 1987).

The Last of the Summer Wine, Roy Clarke (BBC Publications 1976).

Churchill and the Generals, Ian Curteis (BBC Publications, 1980); *The Falklands Play**, (Hutchinson, 1987).

Z Cars, Keith Dewhurst (Longman, 1968). Classic scripts, but note that today series drama is shot on location rather than in the studio.

The Long March, *A Woman Calling*, Ann Devlin (in *Ourselves Alone*, Faber and Faber, 1988).

Hancock's Half Hour, Galton and Simpson (Woburn Press, 1974).

After Pilkington*, Simon Gray (Methuen, 1987).

All Good Men, Trevor Griffiths (Faber and Faber, 1977).

Abel's Will, Christopher Hampton (Faber and Faber, 1979).

Licking Hitler, David Hare (Faber and Faber, 1978); *Dreams of Leaving**, (Faber and Faber, 1980).

Still Waters, Julia Jones (Longman, 1978).

Episodes from 'The Liver Birds', Carla Lane (in *Situation Comedy*, Studio, 1980).

Solid Geometry, Ian McEwan (in *The Imitation Game: Three Plays for Television*, Cape, 1981).

Collected Television Plays, David Mercer (2 vols, John Calder, 1981).

Juliet Bravo, Paula Milne (Longman, 1983). Compare the scene structure and ratio of studio/OB between a *Juliet Bravo* script and a *Z Cars* by Keith Dewhurst or Alan Plater.

Annie Kenny, Alan Plater (in Act Three, Hutchinson, 1979); *Z Cars*, (Longman, 1968).

Pennies From Heaven, Dennis Potter (Quartet Books, 1981). *Waiting for the Boat*, (Faber and Faber, 1984). *The Singing Detective**, (Faber and Faber, 1986).

Bar Mitzvah Boy, *The Evacuees*, *Spend, Spend, Spend*, Jack Rosenthal (in Three Award Winning TV Plays, Penguin, 1978); *Three Plays*, (Penguin, 1986).

Penda's Fen, David Rudkin (Davis-Poynter, 1975).

Our Day Out, Willy Russell (in *Act One*, Hutchinson, 1979).

Soldiers Talking, Cleanly, Mike Stott (Eyre Methuen, 1978).

The Ballard of Ben Bagot, Peter Terson (in *Scene Scripts Two*, Longman, 1978).

BOOKS ON WRITING TV DRAMA

Hazel: the Making of a TV Series, Manuel Alvaredo and Edward Buscombe (BFI/Latimer, 1978).

The TV/Film Script, Rodney Bennett (Harrap, London, 1976). A director's viewpoint.

British Television Drama, George W. Brandt (editor) (Cambridge University Press, 1981).

Writing Comedy for Television, Brian Cooke (Methuen, 1983).

Debut on Two, Phillippa Giles and Vicky Licorish (editors) (BBC Books, 1990). Writers' viewpoints, including Jeanette Winterson on adaptations and Paul Jackson on comedy, plus a script editor's advice from Roger Gregory, a former senior script editor at BBC Pebble Mill, and eight 15-minute plays that featured in the BBC 2 *Debut* series. The editors say: '*Debut on Two* – both the book and the series – aims to inspire new writing for television.' Valuable reading for new writers.

How Plays are Made, Stuart Griffiths (Heinemann Educational, 1982).

Writing for Television and Radio, Robert Hilliard (Focal Press, 1976).

Writing for Television, Malcom Hulke (A & C Black, 1980). Includes television techniques, plotting, dialogue, with excellent examples. (The example of *Three Into One Won't Go* as a characterisation on page 71 comes from this book.)

Writing for Television, Gerald Kelsey (A & C Black, 1990). Covers plots, formats, story construction, dialogue and characterisation, and includes very useful script excerpts from *Howard's Way*, *Brookside* and the film drama *Sun Child* by Angela Huth.

Writing for the BBC, Norman Longmate (BBC Books, 1989). Tells you all about the BBC script unit, which no longer exists, and lists the many programme slots that do not require scripts from outside sources. More a round-up of the BBC's overall output than a useful guide for the new writer. Devotes more space to radio, and in particular local radio, than to television. Of little use until a revised edition appears.

Screenwriting for Narrative Film and Television, William Miller (Columbus Books, London, 1988). Excellent in-depth study of techniques by American film maker and professor.

The Boys from the Blackstuff – the Making of TV Drama, Bob Millington and Rob Nelson (Comedia/Routledge, 1986).

The Way to Write for Television, Eric Paice (Elm Tree Books, 1981). Very good introduction for new writers.

Ah, Mischief: the Writer and Television, Frank Pike (editor) (Faber, 1982). A number of television dramatists including David Edgar put forward their views on the problems of working in television drama.

Television Drama: an Introduction, David Self (Macmillan, 1984).

Play for Today: The Evolution of Television Drama, Irene Shubik (Davis Poynter, 1975).

The Largest Theatre in the World, Shaun Sutton (BBC Publications, 1982). Shaun Sutton, highly respected former head of BBC Television Drama Group, gives a history of British television drama.

Film Scriptwriting: a Practical Manual, Dwight Swain (Focal Press, 1982).

Writing for Television Today, Arthur Swinson (A & C Black, 1965). Gives an account of television drama in its early days, and studies outstanding television plays like *Soldier, Soldier* by John Arden and June Evening by Bill Naughton.

Writing Scripts for Television, Radio and Film, Edgar Willis (Holt, Rinehart and Winston, 1981).

REFERENCE BOOKS

Writers' and Artists' Yearbook (A & C Black) contains general information and lists agents and publishers. It has a section on broadcasting.

The Writers' Handbook edited by Barry Turner (The Macmillan Press), covers markets for radio, film and television scripts.

Index